don't cook
the planet

Emily Abrams

Photography by
Stephen McDonald & Steven Karl Metzer

TRIUMPH
BOOKS

TRIUMPHBOOKS.COM

This book is available in quantity at special dicounts for your group or organization. For further information, contact:

Triumph Books LLC
814 North Franklin Street
Chicago, Illinois 60610
Phone: (312) 337-0747
www.triumphbooks.com

Printed in the USA
ISBN 978-1-60078-972-4

This FSC® certification ensures that all papers in this book were sourced in an environmentally responsible way.

dedication

To my mother for believing in this book and pushing me harder than anyone ever has. You have always stuck by me even when life got busy and stressful. You are an amazing person and an inspiration to all. I love you. Forever and ever.

table of contents

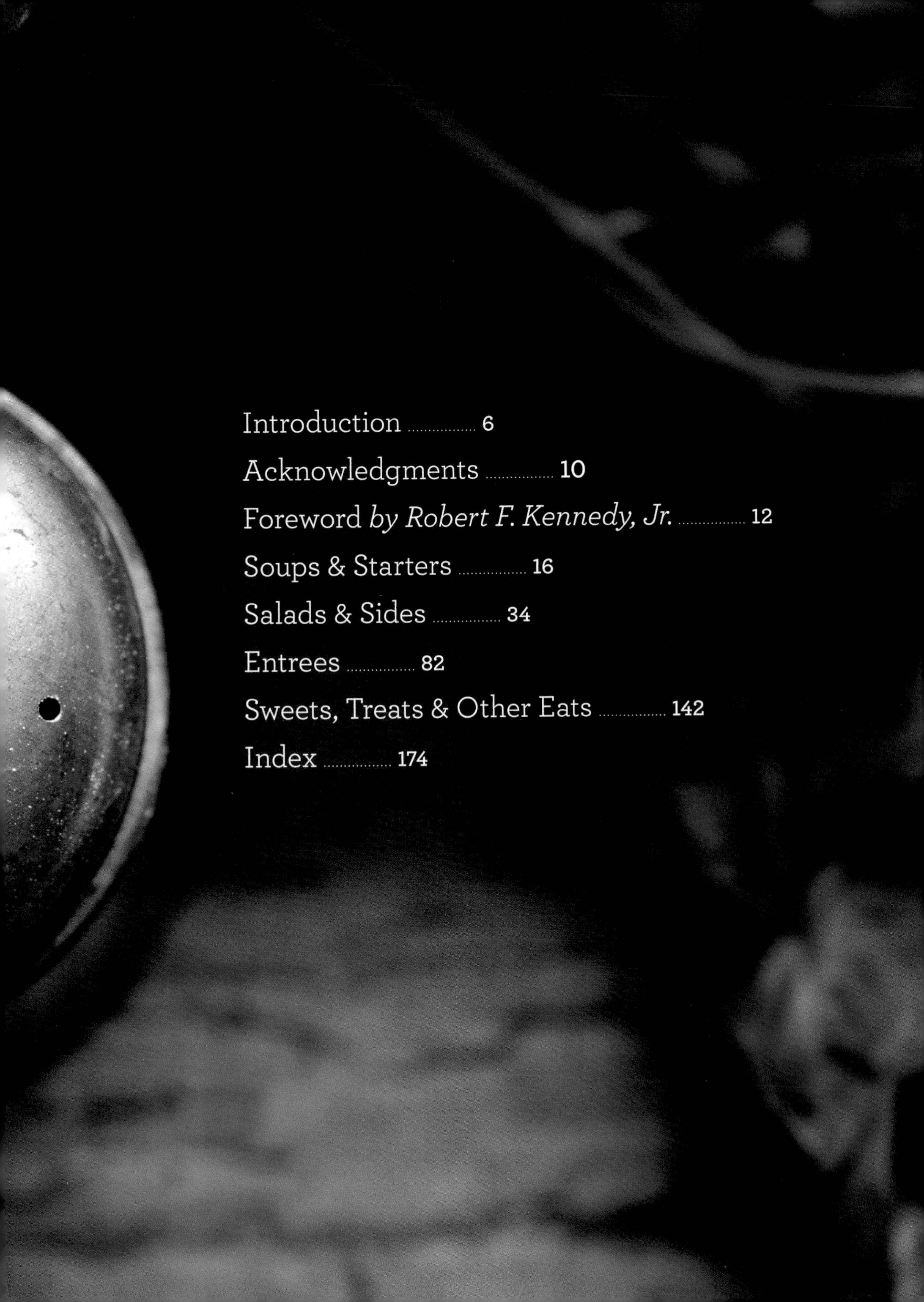

introduction

My name is Emily Abrams; I am 18 years old and a senior at Deerfield Academy, in Deerfield, MA. I am very concerned about global warming and the impact it will have on the planet in the coming decades—from the disruption of weather patterns (which will cause more droughts, floods, and heat waves) to species extinctions and loss of biodiversity. I believe that if this problem goes unchecked **climate change will be the defining issue of my lifetime.**

Climate change is a topic that has been a focal point of many discussions in my household (a household that happens to be powered by geo-thermal energy!). Being vocal about your beliefs and fighting for what is right is something that my parents instilled in me at a very young age. We've grown up fighting to make a difference and to change the world for the better. My mom started a non-profit organization to raise awareness of climate change when I was in grade school. Watching my mother fight to help protect the world in which I hopefully will grow old has given me the desire to do the same.

I've also spent a lot of time over the past few years learning about the environment in my science classes at Deerfield. One course that played a major role in fueling my passion for activism was the AP Cambridge Global Capstone course that specifically focused on water and sustainability. We looked at issues from a local, international and global perspective. My interest in the environment really spiked from this class. I started noticing all of the misconceptions that people had. I was frustrated by the fact that people were unaware of the facts and instead were being told (even by some politicians) that climate change is a hoax.

So what can we do about it? Well, we can all do our part. I wrote this book because I wanted to remind people that climate change isn't just about melting glaciers and dying polar bears. It is a problem that will affect each of us where we live—in our communities, even at our dinner tables. I created this book to show people that the small things you do can help make a difference in the world. And it's easier than most people think.

We think about the food we eat and we make choices—picking foods that are nutritious, or selecting foods in delicious combinations. Everything we eat is a choice. And all of our choices have consequences—if we pick foods that are high in protein, it builds muscles; if we pick foods that are high in sugar, we get quick energy.

Our food choices also affect the planet. Everything we eat has a carbon footprint (or a term I prefer, "carbon foodprint"). Eating locally grown and organic fruits and vegetables will reduce the carbon footprint of the food we eat. Meat has a much higher carbon footprint than fish or chicken; you don't have to be vegan, but perhaps one night each week you might choose to swap a meat dish for a pasta or vegetarian dish.

This book isn't about preaching or aspiring to perfection. This book is simply about mindfulness. It is about empowerment. Knowing that our choices can have a positive impact and doing what we can, when we can.

Eating locally grown foods is not only good for the planet, and good for us—less distance from farm to table means the food is fresher and tastes even better. Throughout this book you will see how chefs, eco-activists, and many celebrities cook or eat sustainably. Doing the right thing for the planet doesn't have to be a trade-off, as you will see from the delicious dishes in this book.

I hope you enjoy the recipes!

Emily Abrams

100%

of the author's proceeds from the sale of this book will be donated to non-profit organizations committed to fighting for a more sustainable planet.

acknowledgments

If you are reading this, I'd like to **thank you** for showing interest in such an important topic. Climate change is a problem that we all face together; no one person can solve it, but together we all can be part of the solution.

Thank you to everyone who participated in the creation of *Don't Cook the Planet*. I especially want to express my gratitude for the people who took the time to share their recipes. From the world-class chefs to environmental leaders, I have been humbled by the outpouring of support for this project. Most importantly, thank you for being role models and not just talking about sustainability, but incorporating it into your work and in your lives.

Gabe Viti, you were the first chef to contribute to the book; not only did you contribute, but you were so enthusiastic that you went out of your way to enlist other chefs, too. (And thank you to Gabe for leading me up Kilimanjaro. You inspire me!) Thank you Bobby for writing the foreword, and for teaching me to speak out and fight for the things we believe in.

To my teachers at Deerfield Academy who have nurtured my thirst for knowledge, and to Mr. Miller who inspired me to pursue learning beyond the classroom— without your guidance on the subject, this book would never have been written. Thank you to Dr. Curtis for giving me the experience of a lifetime at Deerfield.

I had the most wonderful design team. Joline, you are absolutely amazing and we couldn't have put the book together so beautifully without you. Stephen McDonald, Steven Karl Metzer and Abby Lair, your photography is gorgeous. Johanna Lowe, you made everything look perfect—and you made it look easy, too.

Megan Scarsella and Erika Palmer helped with anything and everything. Christine Belgrad, Debbie Berger, Joyce Deep, Wendy Dewey, Lindsay Guetschow, Jessica Lederhausen, Greg Osborn, Remar Sutton, and Dawn Woolen were so nice to reach out to chefs on my behalf. Donna Goodman, Jackie Tate, and the chefs at Miramar, thank you for helping me prepare and test recipes. Katie and Lauren, I love you guys for helping with research, editing, and yes, tasting the recipes!

I was lucky enough to have Triumph Books behind this endeavor, and in particular, thank you to Mitch Rogatz for believing in me.

Finally, thank you to my mom and dad, David, Katie, and Jake for always being there to support and encourage me every step of the way. You guys are the best!

foreword by Robert F. Kennedy, Jr.

On April 22, 1970, twenty million people poured into America's streets to protest the ecological degradation and environmental insults that were impoverishing their quality of life: sooty air, toxic pollution belching from smoke stacks, oil spilled to lakes and oceans, and industrial by-products dumped directly into rivers and streams. Thanks to Rachel Carson's groundbreaking book, *Silent Spring*, some people were also objecting to the poisoning effects of pesticide overuse. Yet it's safe to say that few people would have listed food production among their top environmental concerns.

In fact, though that first Earth Day coincided with the dawn of one of America's biggest environmental disasters: agriculture's industrialization. A seismic shift was taking place away from local food, pasture-based animal husbandry, and traditional farming based on knowledge honed and handed down over the centuries, and toward a food system founded on cruel animal confinement, mechanization, drugs, chemicals, and fossil fuels.

For generations, American farmers had stewarded their lands and animals in ways that largely protected our natural resources. They rotated diverse crops from field to field to keep insect and fungal pests at bay, making chemical pesticides and fungicides unneeded. They raised a variety of farm animals, integrating them into crop rotations to build soil and enhance its fertility, rendering artificial fertilizers unnecessary. Cattle and other grazing animals made good use of non-tillable land as well as being integrated into farming operations to graze fallow fields. Farmers planted grass buffers, tree-lines, and hedgerows to minimize soil erosion. Stalks and husks from grain harvests became animal fodder and bedding. The farm's diverse, cyclical operations preserved, re-used, and restored natural resources affected by food production, safeguarding them for current and future generations.

But farmers who functioned independently and barely used chemical inputs and machinery were problematic for industrialists wanting to convert the food system into a revenue stream. That could only happen if farming and food production became mechanized, consolidated, and vertically integrated. Soon after World War II, assisted by government policies, major corporations began hawking agricultural chemicals and machines while wresting control of America's agriculture from independent farmers and ranchers. Seeds, animal genetics, and slaughter facilities were soon dominated by a small handful of corporations.

Among the most dramatic transformations was pork production. Hundreds of thousands of pig farmers were squeezed out of their livelihoods by agribusiness giants that now control pigs from birth to slaughter. Agricultural economist Dr. John Ikerd has calculated that for every hourly-wage job at a hog factory ten family pig farmers were put out of business. In industrial operations, pigs are crammed into football field–sized metal warehouses, spending their lives deprived of sunlight, exercise, fresh air, or even a soft place to lie down. Their manure is liquefied for ease of transport, making it especially volatile and nauseatingly odiferous. And it is prodigious: the largest industrial hog facilities produce more feces daily than all the humans of New York City combined. The sludge, saturated with antibiotics and a cocktail of other drugs and chemicals, has become a plague of biblical proportions. A single North Carolina spill dumped 25 million gallons of liquefied hog factory manure into rivers and streams, more than twice the amount of oil spilled by the Exxon Valdez.

By the year 2000, the Environmental Protection Agency had declared agriculture the single greatest water polluter, blaming its sediments, nutrients, pathogens, and chemicals for 60 percent of impaired river miles and half of all polluted lake acreage. It's now also a major contributor to climate change and air pollution generally.

But concerns about agriculture go well beyond environmental impacts. Modern food is not only less flavorful (just ask any grandmother how pork or tomatoes tasted when she was a child), it is also far less nourishing. University of Texas research has revealed that over the last half-century, the amounts of protein, calcium, phosphorus, iron, riboflavin and vitamin C in conventionally grown fresh fruits and vegetables have significantly declined. This is the direct result of an industrialized food system where crops are grown in eroded, nutritionally depleted soils, and where crop strains have been deliberately created with vastly longer shelf lives that enable long-distance transport.

While multinational food conglomerates continue erecting animal factories, transporting food an average of 1,200 miles, and using ever more genetically modified crops, survey after survey demonstrate that Americans prefer real food from traditional farms over the products of industrial operations. Consumers consistently say they consider food from family farms safer, healthier, and tastier. They also care about the way animals are treated and the environmental impacts of the food they are eating.

The scale and complexity of our food system can render the task of making it environmentally sustainable and humane seem overwhelming. I've spent much of my time over the past decade suing industrial hog and poultry operations for their water pollution. Simultaneously, I've been pressing Congress and state and federal agencies for stricter enforcement of environmental regulations and statutes. The political paralysis can be discouraging.

Nonetheless, I'm optimistic about the future of our food system. Legal and political action, while valuable, are not the only ways, and are probably not the most important ones, for changing the food system. I've been especially inspired by the young people I've met all over the country—farmers, chefs, urban farmers, community activists, moms—who are taking matters into their own hands and simply building a new and better food system in their communities. They've taught me that even more important than lawsuits and lobbying is what each of us can do, every day, as participants in the food system. By rejecting the products of inhumane and polluting operations, growing some of our own food, and seeking out food from farms that take good care of their land and their animals, each of us can create a better future.

We all have a place in the good food movement. Some of us will be involved in court cases and efforts to improve and enforce our laws. Some of us can start a garden at our home or our child's school. All of us can support good farms and learn to cook. Knowing what to do with those wonderful ingredients once we have them in our hands is another important piece of fixing what ails our broken food system.

That's why I'm so pleased to write the foreword for *Don't Cook the Planet*. I've watched Emily Abrams emerge into one of America's young, imaginative, and energetic environmental leaders who understands that finding a healthier, more delicious way of eating is one type of environmental action we can all enjoy.

soups & starters

chicken soup

Tom Colicchio, founder of Craft Restaurants, judge on *Top Chef*
New York City, NY

1 chicken, quartered, with bones intact (i.e., do not remove breast meat from breastbone, including necks and giblets)
2 carrots, peeled and chopped
2 celery stalks, washed and chopped
2 leeks, washed and chopped
2 parsnips, peeled and chopped
1 onion, peeled and chopped
1 sprig of fresh thyme
Kosher salt, freshly ground black pepper
Coarse sea salt
1½ cups small shell pasta (optional)
Freshly grated Parmigiano-Reggiano (optional)
Extra-virgin olive oil (optional)

This soup is a typical, relaxed, Sunday evening meal for me and my family. I serve this soup the way my grandmother did, with the Parmigiano and olive oil. Every grandmother has a chicken soup recipe, so mine certainly isn't the definitive recipe, but it's still my favorite, and I enjoy sharing that with my kids today the same way my grandmother did with me.

Place 1 gallon water and the chicken in a stockpot and bring to a simmer over medium heat. Simmer gently, skimming regularly, until broth is fragrant, for about 30 minutes.

Add the vegetables and thyme and continue to simmer for another 20 minutes. Season with salt and pepper.

Bring a large pot of salted water to a boil over high heat. Add the pasta and cook until tender, about 8 minutes. Drain and divide the cooked pasta among 4 bowls.

Remove the chicken with a slotted spoon and place on a serving dish. Ladle the broth and vegetables over the pasta and serve with grated Parmigiano, more freshly ground black pepper, and a drizzle of extra-virgin olive oil, if desired. Sprinkle the chicken with coarse sea salt and serve alongside the soup.

chilled english pea soup

Anthony Martin, executive chef, Tru
Chicago, IL

¼ cup finely sliced onion
 Extra-virgin olive oil
1 cup English peas
2 cups vegetable bouillon, heated
½ cup heavy cream
2 teaspoons fresh mint leaves

Sweat onions in olive oil until soft but not brown. Add English peas and cook over medium heat, 2 minutes. Add the hot vegetable bouillon to the peas and onions and bring to a boil, then reduce to a simmer. Cook until peas are just done, about 4 minutes. Do not overcook or soup will discolor. Remove from heat and immediately puree while adding mint and cream. Strain and cool in ice bath. Serve immediately to retain bright green color. Makes 2 servings.

"Natural Resources Defense Council estimates that if all Americans eliminated just one quarter pound serving of beef per week, the reduction in global warming gas emissions would be equivalent to taking four to six million cars off the road."

roasted vegetable bouillon

Wouter Pors, chef, created for Fay Hartog-Levin, former Ambassador to the Kingdom of the Netherlands
The Hague, Netherlands

 2 leeks
 4 carrots
 2 ribs celery
 1 celeriac
 1 large parsnip
 3 onions
 6 cloves garlic
20 pieces shiitake mushrooms
⅓ cup olive oil
 2 branches fresh thyme
 1 bay leaf
10 whole black peppercorns
 2 star anise
10 pieces of whole cardamom pods
 2 lemons, peeled
¾ cup of white wine
 1 tablespoon salt
 8 cups water
 3 Lapsang Souchong single-serve teabags

Preheat the oven to 350°F. Clean and slice the leeks, carrots, celery, celeriac, parsnip, onions, garlic, and shiitake mushrooms into ¾-inch pieces. Put all the vegetables into a big bowl and mix with the olive oil. Place the vegetables into an oven-safe roasting dish and bake in the oven for 15 minutes until golden brown. Place roasted vegetables into a large soup pot. Add the thyme, bay leaf, peppercorns, star anise, cardamom, lemons, white wine, salt, and water. Let simmer for 2 hours on stovetop.

Strain mixture through a cheesecloth; set aside vegetables for another use. Season broth as desired with salt and pepper. Just before serving add the Lapsang Souchong teabags to broth, allowing them to soak for 2-3 minutes, to give that smoky flavor. Do not add teabags until just before serving, otherwise broth becomes bitter.

"We're at a moment in time right now in this country and in the world. We're threatened, all of us, everybody everywhere by the same thing. America is the garden of the world; more things are grown here than any other country in the entire planet. And **the farmers are on the front lines of climate change**. They're living the difference. They love the world, they see the world, they see the climate. They see the sun and the earth, that's what they do. **Farmers today, it is all in their hands**."

—Neil Young speaking at Farm-Aid concert, September 21, 2013
www.farmaid.org

Photo by Abby Lair

salsa fresca

Jan Dee & David Crosby, singer-songwriter
Santa Barbara, CA

4 roma tomatoes, cut into cubes
4 beefsteak tomatoes, cut into cubes
   with juice
1 diced red onion
1 diced Vidalia onion (white or
   yellow)
3 sliced scallions (green onions)
4 cloves garlic, chopped
1 small diced jalapeño pepper
   Serrano peppers (add if you want
   spicy)
   Habanero pepper (be careful, they
   are especially hot)
6 diced greek pepperoncini with
   juice
2 tsp rice wine vinegar
   Juice of 1 lime
   Juice of 1 lemon

**The following should be leaves
only, fresh not dried, and no stems**
1 teaspoon diced cilantro
1 teaspoon diced basil
1 teaspoon diced parsley
1 teaspoon diced dill
1 teaspoon diced oregano

Fold all ingredients together in a large container.

As time goes by, the ingredients will "marry," and every day the taste will alter. It will always become better than it was when first made.

garden gazpacho

**John Englander, oceanographer, author of *High Tide on Main Street*
Boca Raton, FL**

1	46-ounce can of V8 Juice as a base (Use pure vegetable Original or Spicy)
1-2	ripe tomatoes
1	cucumber
1	medium size onion
3	cloves of garlic
1	teaspoon of Worcestershire sauce
	Pepper
	Salt
	Tabasco or other pepper sauce

Pour half can of V8 in blender.

Cut tomatoes, cucumber, and onion in half and put one half in the blender.

Add to the blender:
- garlic
- Worcestershire sauce
- pepper
- salt
- tabasco or other pepper sauce

Blend until smooth, but with chunks of vegetable still visible.

Take half of remaining half of tomatoes, cucumber, and onion and put in blender BRIEFLY to partially blend. Put mix in large bowl or pitcher. Stir in balance of the can of V8.

Dice the remaining quarter of tomatoes, cucumber, and onion to be used as garnish.

Put resulting blend in refrigerator until ready to serve. Put in bowls. Garnish to suit.

tex-mex freshy-fresh guacamole

Edie Brickell & Paul Simon, singer-songwriters
New Canaan, CT

- 1 lime
- 3 ripe organic avocados, peeled, pitted, and cut into large chunks
- 1 small finely chopped organic Vidalia onion
- 1 medium chopped ripe red organic tomato
- 1 medium clove of finely chopped or minced garlic
- ½ teaspoon of sea salt (more or less to taste)
  Pepper
- 2 thin slices of fresh jalapeño, minced or chopped (optional but gives it a nice "bite")
- 1 teaspoon chopped cilantro (optional)

We eat all organic at home and buy from Whole Foods or local farm stands, limiting our meals at restaurants to special occasions.

Eating home-cooked foods and snacks throughout the year, rather than ordering in from restaurants or buying packaged treats, seems to have reduced the number of colds and illnesses we experience, thereby saving on tissues (and packaging/plastics) for a greener existence.

Set your lime aside and mix all other ingredients together until well blended, then cut open your lime and squirt it over the blend. Stir it a few times and serve right away with white or yellow organic sea salted corn chips.

Serves 3 hungry snackers or 5 to 6 nibblers.

Never in a million years did I think that I'd be asked to write a recipe for a book on global warming. I was born and raised in Texas—eating meat at every meal—and recruited by Enron and Exxon during business school. I wasn't a foodie, I wasn't an environmentalist, I wasn't a tree hugger.

Then I had kids—four of them. And as I watched them struggle to eat due to food allergies, and struggle to breathe due to asthma, I was forced to pay attention to something that I had previously dismissed as a hippie thing or a lifestyle of the rich and famous: the environment. Why? Because as the health of my kids started to decline, I learned that they weren't the only ones. They are part of a generation of children that have earned the title "Generation Rx" due to the escalating rates of diseases and conditions impacting them, like the 1 in 3 American kids who now has allergies, asthma, ADHD, or autism. And I didn't like it—what I had to learn, and especially what I had to unlearn. But with four children, I didn't have an option.

So today as I reflect on a request by a high school teenager for a recipe to help save the planet for future generations, I could not be more thankful for this generation and all that they are teaching us. We have to do everything we can to protect the health of our children and the planet we share, because while they may only be 30 percent of the population, they are 100 percent of our future.

—Robyn O'Brien, activist, founder of AllergyKids Foundation

kale chips

Robyn O'Brien, author, activist, founder of AllergyKids Foundation
Los Angeles, CA

1   bunch of kale
2   tablespoon olive oil
¼   teaspoon salt

1 tablespoon lemon juice (optional)
1 tablespoon apple cider vinegar
(optional)
¼ teaspoon cayenne pepper (optional)
¼ teaspoon black pepper (optional)

A friend suggested kale chips. Whatever. Really? Total roughage, was all I could think. But we tried them and got totally hooked. Loaded with nutritional goodness, kale is a powerhouse. And very easy to grow in a backyard garden. This recipe is one that our 8-year-old loves to do on her own. It's that simple.

Preheat oven to 350°F. Rinse kale and chop it into small pieces. Place kale in a large bowl with oil and salt. Add optional ingredients, if desired. With hands, toss and mix ingredients together. Place kale on baking sheet. Bake for about 10-15 minutes (until kale is dark green and crispy).
Cool and serve.

"In 2009, Americans spent $10.6 billion to drink around 8.4 million gallons of water."

Q:

why choose tap water?

Creating plastic bottles consumes energy and money. From pumping the water to manufacturing and transporting bottles, we spend billions of dollars for something that we otherwise have for free coming from our sinks.

According to *The Ripple Effect*, "In 2009, Americans spent $10.6 billion to drink around 8.4 million gallons of just bottled water." To drink eight glasses of tap water a day for an entire year costs around 49 cents for the average New Yorker; the same amount of water costs $1,400 a year for people consuming commercial bottled water.

A study done by Pacific Institute found that it takes about 17 million barrels of oil to create the amount of bottled water that Americans consumed in 2006. That number is equivalent to the amount of energy needed to fuel 1 million American cars and trucks for a year. In contrast, tap water does not require production of plastic bottles, most of which are not properly recycled. In 2006, the polyethylene terephthalate (PET plastics) produced more than 2.5 millions tons of CO_2.

Not only is tap water better for the environment, studies have shown that bottled water is not safer or purer than drinking from the tap in most American cities. According to a study done by the Natural Resources Defense Council, there is no evidence that bottled water is significantly healthier or provides more minerals than tap water. So fill a glass with tap water, and drink to your health!

salads & sides

deconstructed caesar

Graham Elliot, executive chef, Graham Elliot Restaurant Chicago, IL

For the lettuce:
- 3 heads gem lettuce or baby Romaine lettuce

For the Anchoiade Dressing:
- 1 egg yolk
- 1 tablespoon chopped shallot
- 2 cloves garlic
- 2 tablespoons low-fat sour cream
- 1 teaspoon Dijon mustard
- ½ bunch fresh Italian parsley
- 2 tablespoons freshly squeezed lemon juice
- ¾ cup grated Parmesan
- 1 teaspoon anchovy oil
- 1 cup grape seed oil
- 3 tablespoons water (if needed)

For the "Twinkie" filling:
- 2 ounces cream cheese
- 3 ounces mascarpone cheese
- 1 ounce half-and-half
- 2 ounces grated Parmesan
- 1½ teaspoons minced shallot
- 1 tablespoon minced garlic
- Salt to taste

Brioche twinkie
- ½ loaf of uncut brioche Pullman (square loaf)
- ½ cup butter

For the Parmesan fluff:
- 4 ounces Parmigiano-Reggiano

For the garniture:
- 12 fillets Spanish anchovy
- Freshly ground black pepper

For the lettuce:
Cut two-thirds of the way down from the top of the lettuce. Discard the upper part or reserve it for another use. Cut the bottom one-third of the lettuce into 4 equal pieces. Repeat with the remaining 2 heads of lettuce.

Soak all pieces in cold water to remove any dirt. Pat dry and place in a bowl for serving.

For the Anchoiade Dressing:
In a high speed blender, place all ingredients except for Parmesan, oils, and water. Puree until smooth. Add Parmesan and puree for 1 minute. Slowly add oils in a small steady stream while blender is running. Pause every 10 seconds to make sure oil is fully incorporated.

If the dressing gets too thick, adjust consistency with a touch of water.

For the "Twinkie" filling:
In a food processor, combine all ingredients and mix until fully incorporated. Using a rubber spatula, fill a pastry bag with the mixture. Reserve for later.

Brioche twinkie
Using a serrated knife, remove all of the crust from the bread. Cut 1 × 3-inch rectangles from the brioche.

Melt the butter in a small saucepot. Brush all sides of the bread rectangles with melted butter.

In a nonstick sauté pan, gently brown the rectangles on medium heat. Remove rectangles from pan and rest on a paper towel to soak up any excess butter.

For the Parmesan fluff:
Using a microplane, carefully grate the Parmigiano-Reggiano over a bowl.

For the assembly:
Use a rounded spoon end to hollow out two holes in the breadsticks.

Pipe in the "Twinkie" filling until each breadstick is stuffed full. Place breadsticks on a cookie sheet and bake in the oven at 350°F for 3 minutes to warm the center.

Using a paintbrush, coat each piece of lettuce generously with dressing and roll in Parmesan fluff. Place each breadstick on a plate and gently rest 3 pieces of lettuce atop.

Garnish with a Spanish anchovy on each piece of lettuce and freshly ground black pepper.

"**Locavore:** A person whose diet consists only or principally of **locally grown or produced foods.**"

—Oxford Dictionary

garlic vinaigrette

Alice Waters, author, activist, chef/proprietor of Chez Panisse Restaurant Berkeley, CA

1 small garlic clove
  Salt
2 tablespoons red wine vinegar
  Fresh-ground black pepper
3 to 4 tablespoons olive oil

Garlic vinaigrette is the dressing I make most often. The quantities listed are only an approximate guide because garlics, vinegars, and oils vary so much in strength and intensity. The first step in making a vinaigrette is to macerate garlic in vinegar and salt. The vinegar softens the raw taste of the garlic, and the salt tames the sharp edge of the vinegar. Sometimes I like to mix different kinds of vinegar; a few drops of balsamic vinegar can temper a wine vinegar that's too strong. Taste for balance and adjust by adding more salt or vinegar; it should be neither too salty nor too acidic. The mixture should taste delicious by itself.

Put a peeled garlic clove and 2 big pinches of salt in a mortar and pound into a purée with no chunks remaining. Add the wine vinegar, grind in some black pepper, and taste for the balance of salt and vinegar. Allow to macerate for a few minutes, and whisk in olive oil. Taste the dressing with a leaf of lettuce. It should taste bright and lively without being too acidic or too oily; adjust the salt, vinegar, or oil as needed. Makes 4 servings.

To dress a salad, put several generous handfuls of washed and dried lettuce in a large bowl. Toss with about three quarters of the vinaigrette, and taste. The lettuce should be lightly coated but not overdressed; add more dressing as needed.

Use a finely diced shallot instead of, or in addition to, the garlic paste.

A squeeze of lemon juice added to the dressed salad at the last moment can add a brightness that brings up all the flavors.

"What we are calling for is a revolution in public education—the Delicious Revolution. When the hearts and minds of our children are captured by a school lunch curriculum, enriched with experience in the garden, sustainability will become the lens through which they see the world."

— Alice Waters

sundance salad

Robert Redford, actor, director, founder of Sundance Film Festival Sundance, UT

Salad
  Artisan Greens
  Soaked Dried Currants
  Candied Pecans (see recipe)
  Herbed Goat Cheese (Drake Family
    Farms)
  Sherry Vinaigrette (see recipe)

Sherry Vinaigrette
  1   shallot, sliced
  1   3-inch sprig fresh thyme leaves
  ½   cup sherry vinegar
  1   teaspoon Dijon mustard
  1   teaspoon honey
  1   cup blended oil

Candied Pecans
  1   cup pecan halves
  ½   cup powdered sugar
  Oil for deep frying
  1   pinch cayenne
  1   pinch salt

For vinaigrette, add all ingredients except the oil in a blender. While blender is on high, slowly add oil to emulsify.

For candied pecans, blanch pecans in boiling water. Remove from water and place in mixing bowl. Add powdered sugar and stir to coat. Deep fry pecans at 375°F until they no longer bubble, approximately 5-8 minutes. Remove and sprinkle with cayenne and salt.

Toss greens, currants, and pecans with vinaigrette. Top with goat cheese.

"I think the environment should be put in the category of our national security. Defense of our resources is just as important as defense abroad. Otherwise what is there to defend?"

— Robert Redford

I am so happy that you are doing something to raise the awareness of global warming and sustainability of food sources. I love to cook and I have four sons who might want to become chefs one day as well. My hope is that they will have the same opportunity to cook the same foods that I grew up cooking. I also love to fish; however, I always "catch and release" which returns the fish back into the water. I also hope my youngest son will one day get to fish and enjoy the ocean's bounty.

   We as a company love to support our local farmers for so many reasons: The food just tastes better. The farmers use less gas and auto emissions to get the food to us. We keep the money close to home to help support our local economy. Also, we feel good about helping folks we know rather than a big nameless faceless mainline company.

   From the bottom of my heart, thank you so much for your efforts. Great luck to you!

—John Chiakulas

farmers market greens, grilled vegetables, tomatoes & basil

John Chiakulas, corporate executive chef of Lettuce Entertain You Enterprises

Salad

3½ cups local baby lettuces
    and mesclun mix
 1 cup grilled zucchini and yellow
    squash
 ½ cup grilled sweet red peppers
 ½ cup ripe assorted tomato wedges
 1 teaspoon plus 1 pinch julienned
    fresh basil
1½ ounces Market Vinaigrette
    (see recipe)
 1 pinch kosher salt and pepper mix

Market Vinaigrette

1½ cups light olive oil
 ¼ cup white balsamic vinegar
 ¼ cup fresh squeezed lemon juice
 1 pinch kosher salt and pepper mix
 ½ tablespoon sugar
 5 to 6 turns freshly ground black
    pepper
 2 tablespoons water

Toss greens with sliced grilled squash and peppers, tomato wedges, 1 teaspoon basil, Market Vinaigrette, and salt and pepper.

Pile salad high on plate, pulling out vegetables to scatter over top.

Sprinkle top with pinch of julienned basil. Makes 1 serving.

Market Vinaigrette

In a mixing bowl, add all ingredients. Whisk to combine (do not blend).

Place in a glass jar, label, and refrigerate. Makes about 2 cups.

farme
marke

FRESH
MICHIGAN
RED HAVEN
PEACHES
6.00/C

Photo by Emily Abrams

Cities in North America are undergoing a food revolution! As urban areas developed throughout our history, we built on agricultural land. In this process, cities have traditionally received food from rural areas and taken our waste back. As we've lost urban agricultural land to sprawling suburbs, we've needed to look farther afield for our produce. Now, the average piece of food travels over 2,000 miles from farm to plate, contributing to greenhouse gas emissions, lower nutrition, and cities that are vulnerable to disruptions in transportation systems.

Cities, their residents, businesses, and non-profits are now investing in growing, distributing, and processing food within their communities. Municipal governments are playing an important role in enabling this transformation by removing barriers in building and zoning codes, as well directly supporting it, with grants and access to land.

The barriers that exist in many cities have been around for a long time and take time to change, but cities are investing the time to bring about change. For instance in the city of Vancouver, the City Council recently changed the zoning code to make it easier and cheaper to host a farm market in any part of the city. As a result the number of farmers markets virtually doubled within a year.

To incentivize growing, distributing and processing food in our communities, cities are playing an active role by providing grants and land, as well as purchasing local foods for their own operations. For instance in Vancouver the city has made several acres of land available to a non-profit called Sole Food, which has hired hard-to-employ residents to grow food. Over a two-year period, urban farming has increased from 4 to 8 acres in the city.

By supporting and investing in urban agriculture, cities across North America are ushering in a new era in urban eating and being involved with their food, which is making our communities more resilient and healthier. City dwellers are raising chickens in their backyards, installing bee hives on their roof tops, growing veggies in their front yards, getting to know their neighbors at farmers markets, and enjoying locally grown goods from food carts. It's truly an exciting time to be involved in food in our cities.

— Sadhu A. Johnston, LEED AP Deputy City Manager
City of Vancouver, BC

farmers market greens, peaches & pecan salad

**John Chiakulas, corporate executive chef of
Lettuce Entertain You Enterprises
Chicago, IL**

Salad
- 3 cups local baby lettuces and mesclun mix
- 1 cup sliced fresh local peaches
- ½ cup grilled sweet corn
- 2 ounces Market Vinaigrette (see recipe)
- 1 pinch kosher salt and pepper mix
  Roasted pecans

Market Vinaigrette
- 1½ cups light olive oil
- ¼ cup white balsamic vinegar
- ¼ cup fresh squeezed lemon juice
- 1 pinch kosher salt and pepper mix
- ½ tablespoon sugar
- 5 to 6 turns freshly ground black pepper
- 2 tablespoons water

Always wash and sanitize hands, work area, and utensils prior to starting task.

Toss greens with peaches, grilled corn, Market Vinaigrette, and salt and pepper.

Pile salad high on plate, pulling out peaches and corn to scatter over top.

Sprinkle top with roasted pecans..

Market Vinaigrette
In a mixing bowl, add all ingredients. Whisk to combine (do not blend).

Place in a glass jar, label, and refrigerate. Makes about 2 cups.

panzanella salad

David DiGregorio, executive chef, Osteria Via Stato Restaurant
Chicago, IL

4   slices ciabatta bread, cut into
      1-inch slices
2   tablespoons olive oil plus 3
      tablespoons extra-virgin olive oil
4   cloves garlic, halved
2   cups sweet Sun Gold or heirloom
      cherry tomatoes
1   cup farmers market cucumbers,
      peeled, cut in half, seeds removed,
      and sliced thin
2   teaspoons sweet onion, slivered
3   teaspoons fresh basil, torn
2   teaspoons Cerignola olives,
      slivered
1   ounce red wine vinegar
      Salt and pepper to taste

Drizzle ciabatta slices with the 2 tablespoons olive oil and toast on sheet tray in 500°F oven with fan on for 5 to 6 minutes or until golden brown. After toasted, rub each slice with the cut side of a garlic clove, then tear slices into 1-inch pieces.

In a large bowl, combine bread with 3 tablespoons olive oil, red wine vinegar, and remaining ingredients. Taste and adjust seasoning with salt and pepper, if needed.

Arrange on plate and serve.

"When buying food at the store, look at how it's packaged. For example: buy eggs in cartons that are cardboard rather than styrofoam, buy milk in recyclable glass bottles, and buy dried fruits, nuts, and grains in bulk instead of individually wrapped."

Photo courtesy of Osteria Via Stato Restaurant

hickory hill deviled eggs

Ethel Kennedy
Hyannisport, MA

½   teaspoon Worcestershire sauce
1   teaspoon lemon juice
1   teaspoon Dijon mustard
½   teaspoon curry powder
    Salt
½   cup Greek yogurt
    Parsley for garnish
    Bacon bits to top
    Eggs (dozen)

Hard boil eggs. Peel eggs carefully from shell and slice lengthwise. Remove egg yolks and mix with listed ingredients until mostly smooth. Spoon mixture into egg white halves. Sprinkle bacon bits on top if desired and garnish with parsley.

roasted cauliflower

Stephanie Izard, winner of *Top Chef*, executive chef, Girl & the Goat Restaurant
Chicago, IL

Roasted Cauliflower:
- 2 tablespoons oil
- 4 cups cauliflower, sliced
  Salt
- 2 tablespoons water
- 1 teaspoon Crunch Butter
  (see recipe)
- 1 tablespoon pine nuts, toasted
- 2 tablespoons pickled peppers
- 1 ounce Parmesan cheese, grated
- 1 tablespoon fresh mint, torn

For Crunch Butter:
- 4 ounces unsalted butter, softened
- 1 clove garlic, grated
- 2 tablespoons Parmesan cheese, grated
- 2 tablespoons Panko bread crumbs
  Salt

For garnish:
- 2 teaspoons pine nuts, toasted
- 2 teaspoons Parmesan cheese, grated
- 2 teaspoons fresh mint, torn

Heat oil in a sauté pan. Add cauliflower, tossing and cooking until caramelized on all sides. Season with salt.

Add water and steam cauliflower until cooked.

Add the Crunch Butter and toss to coat. Then add the pine nuts and pickled peppers. Toss until heated.

Remove from heat. Add the Parmesan cheese and mint. Toss to combine. Platter or plate as desired and garnish with pine nuts, Parmesan cheese, and mint. Makes 4 servings.

For Crunch Butter:
In a mixer fitted with a paddle attachment, combine all the ingredients and whip until light and fluffy.

warm white & green Michigan asparagus with aged parmesan & poached egg

J. Joho, chef/proprietor of Everest, Eiffel Tower Restaurant, Brasserie JO, Paris Club
Chicago, IL

2	bunches white asparagus
2	bunches green asparagus
8	farm-raised organic chicken eggs
½	quart milk
1	tablespoon butter
1	lemon, juiced
	Salt and pepper
2	tablespoons olive oil
6	ounces aged Parmesan, shredded
	Espelette seasoning

Preheat oven to 350 degrees. Trim off ends of white and green asparagus, and peel the stalks. Set bunches aside.

In a stockpot mix milk, 1 tablespoon butter, lemon juice, and salt over medium heat. Add white asparagus; allow to simmer until al dente and then remove. Poach eggs in same pot and set aside.

Meanwhile, drizzle green asparagus with 1 tablespoon olive oil, salt, and pepper, then spread onto baking sheet and roast 5-10 minutes until tender.

Arrange white and green asparagus on 8 plates. Drizzle each dish with remaining olive oil, sprinkle with shaved aged Parmesan, and season with salt and pepper. Top each plate with one poached egg and finish with a dash of Espelette seasoning. Serve immediately.

Photo courtesy of Everest Restaurant

cucumbers with pasta

Tom Martin, former horticulturalist for the Illinois Governor's Mansion Springfield, IL

Cold Cucumber-Tomato Topping
- 1 pound cucumbers
  Salt and freshly ground pepper
  White wine vinegar
- 1½ pound very ripe tomatoes
- ½ cup red onions, chopped
- 1 teaspoon minced garlic
- 2 tablespoon chopped parsley
- 1 tablespoon chopped fresh basil
- ¼ cup olive oil
- 1 pound spaghetti
  Grated Parmesan cheese

Cold Cucumber-Tomato topping for pasta

This topping can be made ahead of time and refrigerated but bring to room temperature before tossing with pasta.

Peel and seed the cucumbers. Dice the flesh into ¼ inch pieces, and toss with ½ teaspoon salt and 2 tablespoons wine vinegar. Let sit for 30 minutes, and drain.
Peel, seed, and dice the tomatoes, and combine with the cucumbers, onions, garlic, herbs, and olive oil. Taste and add more vinegar, salt, and pepper if necessary.

Boil the spaghetti in several quarts of salted water until cooked. Toss the hot pasta with the cucumber-tomato mixture. Serve with grated Parmesan cheese.

In my youth, tending to the family vegetable garden was a chore that my brothers and I were required to perform. What once seemed as forced labor is now a passion and labor of love.

Although vegetable gardening may seem intimidating to most people, my opinion is that the learning curve is not nearly as steep as ornamental horticulture. Requirements for successful vegetables are sun, soil, and space. Full sun or at least six hours of sun is absolutely essential. Good soil is also essential, and the use of raised beds with well-drained soil amended with a generous amount of compost or organic matter will achieve the best results. When space is limited, careful consideration must be given to what crops to grow and what the space requirements are for those crops. If space is limited, plants such as tomatoes, peppers, eggplant, and basil can be grown in containers placed on a patio or balcony.

Vegetables can be categorized as either cool-season or warm-season crops. Although some cool-season crops such as lettuce can be grown throughout the growing season, warm-season crops such as tomato, squash, pepper and eggplant will not tolerate cool temperatures. Along with lettuce, other cool-season crops are spinach, cabbage, broccoli, cauliflower, onion, radish, carrots, beets and peas. These cool-season crops can be planted in early spring. Almost all vegetable plants can be started from seed sown directly in the soil or started indoors. Seed packets give all the necessary information for sowing. Many garden centers and even big box stores now sell individual plants, which is very practical. Along with weeding, most maintenance consists of staking or caging tomatoes. Some crops such as cucumber, peas, and beans can be grown as climbers on a trellis.

Fresh herbs such as basil, parsley, sage, chives, thyme, and oregano can easily be grown in containers, and may even be grown on a window sill. Consider space requirements for container size and remember that full sun is necessary. Purchase a prepared potting soil mix for use in containers.

After a few seasons, vegetable gardening will become easy and very rewarding.

—Tom Martin

BLT salad

Beau MacMillan, *Iron Chef America* winner, executive chef, Sanctuary on Camelback Mountain
Phoenix, AZ

3 medium size heirloom tomatoes (different varieties and color)
1 tablespoon chives, chopped
1 teaspoon tarragon, chopped
1 teaspoon chervil, chopped
  Olive oil
1 slice brioche bread
1 tablespoon clarified butter
1 teaspoon pepper spice (recipe follows)
2 strips bacon, cooked
½ cup tempura batter (recipe below)
  Half of an avocado, cut into thirds
4 ounces arugula, fried crisp

Pepper Spice
2 tablespoons paprika
2 tablespoons black pepper, crushed
2 tablespoons pink pepper
2 tablespoons Kosher Salt
1 tablespoon granulated garlic
1 tablespoon granulated onion
1 tablespoon coriander, crushed
1 tablespoon dill
1 tablespoon red pepper flakes, crushed

Tempura Batter
1 cup rice flour
1 cup carbonated water

BLT Dressing
1 cup buttermilk
1 cup mayonnaise
½ cup bacon, cooked and chopped
1 cup spinach, chopped
¼ cup tomato jam (recipe follows)
1 whole shallot, chopped

1 teaspoon garlic, chopped
  Salt and pepper to taste

Tomato Jam (for BLT Dressing)
1 pound vine ripe tomatoes
2 oranges
½ cup sugar
½ teaspoon togarashi (Japanese chili spice)
1 ounce soy sauce
½ cup water
2 ounces red wine vinegar

Directions

Wash and core heirloom tomatoes. Rough chop the tomatoes and season with chopped herbs. Drizzle tomatoes with extra-virgin olive oil and salt and pepper.

Chop the 2 strips of bacon and fold into tomatoes. Mix ingredients for Pepper Spice.

Cut edges off brioche bread to form a square, about 2 × 2 inches. Brush brioche with clarified butter and season with Pepper Spice. Bake in 300°F oven until golden and toasted like a crouton.

Dip avocado into Tempura Batter and fry till crispy. Mix ingredients for BLT Dressing.

On a 12-inch plate dollop 2 ounces of BLT Dressing and place crouton over the top. Place the marinated tomatoes and bacon on top with the tempura avocado. Spoon over a little more BLT Dressing and garnish with fried arugula.

Directions for Tempura Batter
Take the carbonated water and gradually pour over the rice flour to achieve a pancake batter consistency. Once ready you will dip the avocado into the Tempura Batter and fry till crispy.

Directions for Tomato Jam
Remove peel from tomatoes and finely chop. Place in sauce pan with all other ingredients and bring to a boil. Cook rapidly, stirring often until liquid has evaporated by 80% and tomato has jam-like consistency. Refrigerate and use as needed.

Grow your own spices: Basil and oregano are easy to grow in your home garden and easy to pot on your kitchen window sill. Not only are you reducing your carbon footprint by completely eliminating the distance from farm to table but there is nothing better than home grown spices straight from your backyard.

"I would have to say the biggest issue of global warming for us is the effect on the shellfish here in the Puget Sound. The acidification of the ocean due to the rise of carbon dioxide in the atmosphere has made it so that oysters do not grow wild in certain parts of our area. This is so wrong on so many levels and needs to be stopped. The only way we can do that is one action at a time pushing in the right direction. It has taken us many, many years to get to this point and to reverse course will take the same amount of effort. I know we are on the right track, and we will make it right for future generations to come."

—Joshua Henderson

kale caesar

Joshua Henderson, chef and founder of The Skillet Group
Seattle, WA

For the dressing:
- 2 small cloves garlic, minced and mashed to a paste with ¼ teaspoon salt
- 1 teaspoon anchovy paste
- 2 tablespoons fresh lemon juice
- 1 teaspoon lemon zest
- 1 teaspoon Dijon-style mustard
- 1 teaspoon Worcestershire sauce
- 1 cup mayonnaise
- ½ cup freshly grated Parmesan
- 1 teaspoon coarse freshly ground black pepper

For the croutons:
- 4 cups day-old bread cut into 1-inch cubes
- 3 tablespoons olive oil
- 1 teaspoon each salt and pepper

For the salad:
- 6 cups chopped dinosaur kale or organic kale
- 1 cup dressing
- 8 each boquerones (or fresh anchovies)
- 1½ cups croutons

Toss bread cubes with olive oil and seasoning. Bake in 350°F oven for 10 minutes or until golden brown.

Toss kale with dressing and place on four plates. Allow kale to stand tall as it is naturally fluffy. Scatter croutons and top with 2 boquerones in an X pattern.

roasted broccoli & live oats

**Steve Ells, founder, co-CEO of Chipotle
Denver, CO**

For the live oats:
- 1 cup live oats from Cayuga Organics
- 1½ cups water
- 1 teaspoon kosher salt
- 1 tablespoon extra-virgin olive oil

For the broccoli:
- 6 broccoli heads, stems included
- 1 cup walnuts, toasted and crushed

For the garnish:
- 2 apples, cut into ⅛-inch-thick slices
- 1 cup Parmesan, shaved or grated
  Freshly squeezed lemon juice
- 2 tablespoons extra-virgin olive oil

For the live oats:

Rinse live oats under running water in a mesh strainer, moving oats in a circular motion. Live oats are naturally hull-less, so the goal is to rinse away any sediment. Bring 1½ cups water to a boil with the 1 teaspoon of salt in a medium-size pot. Pour live oats into the boiling water. Reduce heat, bringing the water to a simmer. Cook for 30-45 minutes until tender. Drain and coat the oats in 1 tablespoon extra-virgin olive oil.

For the broccoli:

Preheat oven to 300°F. Toast walnuts on a sheet tray for approximately 10-15 minutes or until golden brown. Set aside to cool.

Increase oven temperature to 425°F. Peel broccoli stems. Grate 2 heads of raw broccoli into a salad bowl. Reserve the stems for roasting. You can use a mandoline to do the grating but be extremely careful with the blade. You can achieve the same effect with a box grater or with a knife—if your knife skills are up to par. Season broccoli with salt and olive oil and arrange on sheet tray.

Slice broccoli stems in half lengthwise, season with salt and pepper, and arrange on separate sheet trays. Place trays in oven for approximately 10-15 minutes or until well cooked. Broccoli should be well browned. Do not fear caramelization! Caramelization is the process of concentrating the vegetables' natural sugars, creating a golden brown exterior. Remove trays from oven and set aside to cool.

Mix all ingredients in large salad bowl, garnish with apples, Parmesan, and lemon juice, and serve.

CHIPOTLE'S PHILOSOPHY

It's all fun and games until someone wrecks a planet

Industrial ranching and factory farming produce tons of waste while depleting the soil of nutrients. These seem like bad things to us. So we work hard to source our ingredients in ways that protect this little planet of ours.

Organic food is food as it was meant to be grown or raised. It's a pretty big word these days, but it's not always pretty. Organic produce, for example, can be smaller in size and look less appetizing than its non-organic counterparts. Still, we believe food raised organically benefits people and the environment, and we know it tastes better.

Currently, 40% of our beans are organically grown, which has a number of benefits including a reduction of more than 140,000 pounds of chemical pesticide since 2005. We have been increasing our use of organically grown beans over the last few years and may use even more in the coming years.

Organic is great, but it's not always appropriate for the food we serve. Sometimes we can find farmers who focus on responsible or sustainable practices but aren't certified organic. We make that call market-by-market, ingredient-by-ingredient, always keeping the big picture in mind.

Family farms are slowly disappearing, but we're doing our best to keep that from happening. At Chipotle, we prefer working with farms that are family owned and operated. We like the idea of family farms, but we also believe the foods they grow taste better.

Family farmers take great care to respect their farmland because it's the only land

they have. If they plant one crop over and over that depletes the nutrients in the soil, they're the ones who suffer. Family farmers rotate crops, plant multiple crops, avoid pesticides and generally farm in a sustainable way.

But just because a farm is small or family owned doesn't mean it meets our standards. That's why we spend a lot of time meeting and speaking with each of our suppliers to ensure we're all on the same page.

Local: The less distance food has to travel, the better. It just makes sense. Sourcing local food reduces food miles, supports rural economies, and ensures fresh, great-tasting seasonal produce.

mom's spinach soufflé

Wendy Abrams, founder of Cool Globes (a.k.a. my mom)
Highland Park, IL

4 cups chopped fresh spinach (if fresh is not available, use 2 boxes of 8 oz chopped frozen spinach)
5 eggs
¾ cup chopped onions
2 cups cottage cheese
½ cup shredded asiago cheese
¼ cup shredded cheddar cheese
Salt
Pepper

Preheat oven to 400 degrees.

Mix spinach, eggs, onions, and cottage cheese in mixing bowl; add asiago cheese and mix together.

Throw in pinch of salt and pepper.

Pour mixture into greased 7 × 11 inch baking dish.

Sprinkle shredded cheddar across the top.

Bake (approximately 1 hour) until top is golden brown.

"Fortunately for Emily, she is a much better cook than her mother. I have a few fall-back recipes that are easy and everyone enjoys; this is one of them. **We grew spinach and onions in our garden this summer and making soufflé with homegrown ingredients was the best.**

With regard to eating sustainably, we are nowhere near perfect, but we're mindful. **Perhaps as important as the food on the table, is the conversation around it.** Our kids have a keen sense of awareness of the world around them, and for that I am tremendously grateful."

—Wendy Abrams

Photo by Abby Lair

Eating Seasonally

As the seasons change, so does our metabolism. It appears that Mother Nature may know best. During the different seasons, not only are your nutritional needs different, foods affiliated with a particular season affect your body quite differently.

Here are some general guidelines you can follow to ensure optimal nourishment in every season:

In fall, turn to more warming, autumn harvest foods, such as onions, garlic, carrots, and sweet potatoes. Apples are particularly cleansing in the fall months. Also liberally use more warming spices such as ginger, cayenne, peppercorns, and mustard seeds.

In winter, focus even more exclusively on consuming warming foods that take longer to grow than cooling foods that grow quickly. Root vegetables are especially warming, as are animal protein such as fish, chicken, beef, and lamb. In addition, corn, nuts, and eggs are all warming.

In spring, consume the dark leafy vegetables that represent the fresh new growth of this season. The greening that occurs in springtime should be represented by greens on your plate, including Swiss chard, Romaine lettuce, dandelion, fresh parsley, and basil.

In summer, stick with light, cooling foods recommended in traditional Chinese medicine. These foods include strawberries, blueberries, apples, pears, plums, summer squash, broccoli, cauliflower, asparagus, green beans, peppermint, and cilantro.

During winter, the external conditions turn windy, dry, and cold, so do your internal conditions, which means a diet containing moist and warm foods that naturally nourish you.

In all seasons, be creative! Let the natural backdrop of fall, winter, spring, and summer be your guide.

To your good health!

—Karen Malkin, Health Counselor

quinoa cakes

**Kirstin Uhrenholdt & Laurie David, co-authors of *The Family Dinner*
Los Angeles, CA**

Quinoa Cakes:

- 2 eggs
- ¼ cup flour
- 3 tablespoons tahini, almond butter, or peanut butter
- 1 tablespoon red or white wine vinegar
- 3 cups cooked quinoa
- ¼ cup finely diced onion
- 2 garlic cloves minced
- 1 cup finely grated sweet potato (this is a secret ingredient, it holds the batter together)
- 1 (10-ounce) box frozen chopped spinach, thawed and squeezed dry
- ½ cup chopped nuts (pine nuts, walnuts, or your favorite nuts), optional
- ½ cup chopped sun-dried tomatoes
- 4 ounces crumbled feta cheese
- 2 tablespoons chopped parsley, dill, or cilantro
- 1 teaspoon salt
  Black pepper, cumin, and/or cayenne to taste
  Vegetable or grape seed oil

Quick Roasted Red Pepper Sauce:

- 1½ cups drained fire-roasted red peppers from a jar
- ½ cup toasted almonds
- 2 teaspoons red wine vinegar
  Salt and pepper to taste

We are huge fans of our quinoa cakes. They are crispy, crunchy, and tasty—perfect for Meatless Mondays—and they are great for using up veggie leftovers! Just take this recipe and replace the spinach with any cooked vegetable you have in the fridge: some of your leftover black beans, sautéed mushrooms, or a cup of Sunday's roasted vegetables chopped up. All would be fabulous!

And this is just the beginning. Next time, throw in some lentils and curry and call them Indian koftas. Or add a bunch of parsley and stuff them into pita bread with lettuce and tahini sauce. Now you have a healthy quinoa falafel! Hurrah! It's a whole world of quinoa cake possibilities! Allow the kids to help! They can peel and grate the sweet potato, mix mix mix, and patty-cake the quinoa cakes into shape.

Quinoa Cakes

In your favorite mixing bowl mix the first 4 ingredients, then add all the other ingredients except the oil. Stir until everything is well combined. Let the mixture chill in the fridge for about a ½ hour.

Preheat your oven to 400°F.

Make the quinoa cakes by placing 3-4 tablespoons of the mixture into your wet hands and firmly forming it into a round flat "patty," then put it onto a well-oiled baking sheet.

Bake, flipping halfway through, until lightly browned and just crisp, about 25 minutes. Serve with quick roasted red pepper sauce (see recipe below), tzatziki, chutney, or tomato sauce.

Quick Roasted Red Pepper Sauce

Put all the ingredients in a blender and blend until smooth.

mushrooms with garlic & parsley

HRH Prince Philippe de Bourbon-Parme
Lejre, Denmark

Porcino mushrooms (Portobello
  mushrooms can be used if you
  cannot get hold of Porcino)
1 lemon
2 to 3 cloves garlic
2 to 3 tablespoons fresh parsley,
  chopped (or 1 tablespoon dried
  parsley)
Salt
Pepper
Olive oil
Whipping cream (optional)

Clean the mushrooms and chop them in chunks. You can also cut them into ¼-inch slices cutting from the top to bottom.

Add oil to the fying pan, add the mushrooms, salt, and pepper. Simmer at low heat until the fluid has evaporated. The mushrooms emit a lot of fluid.

Add chopped garlic. I usually make a small space in the middle of the frying pan. Add a teaspoon of oil and place the garlic in the space until the garlic pieces are clear.

Mix the mushrooms and garlic, and add the juice of ½ a lemon or a little more. (According to taste). Simmer for a while more and add the fresh parsley just before serving.

If you are using dried parsley, add this at the same time as the lemon juice.

If you want a richer taste, add whipping cream and simmer the whole lot a few minutes more.

Delicious, serve with meat or bird. And remember—do not tell where you found your mushrooms.

My family has an old tradition of collecting wild mushrooms in the forests around Ledreborg palace in Denmark. Since I was a small boy I went out with my mother to collect the various wild fungi one can find, especially in the fall.

From childhood we learned to identify which mushrooms were good to eat, and which would kill you if you ate them.

Our search was—and still is—a game of hide and seek: my branch of the family jealously guards the location of our small treasure places from other family branches!

One of the better mushrooms is *Boletus Edulis*, known as Penny Bun, Porcino, or Cep.

The Penny Bun is a large, tasty mushroom eagerly hunted in many countries. However, I never really found a satisfying way to cook them. The Penny Bun became a bit slimy and bland when cooked.

This all changed when I met a tall, dark and beautiful French woman. She had grown up in the Pyrenees mountains in France, and spent time with her grandmother hunting for mushrooms. She gave me this recipe that was passed down from mother to child.

- HRH Prince Philippe de Bourbon-Parme

Reducing your Carbon "Foodprint"

Many people don't realize how easily they can make a difference, simply by reducing their carbon footprint. Our food's carbon footprint (or as I like to say, the "carbon foodprint") is measured by the amount of greenhouse gas emissions produced through growing, rearing, farming, processing, transporting, storing, cooking, and disposing of the food on your plate. While each household's carbon footprint is different, a good amount of it is made up from the carbon footprint of food.

Up to one-fifth of the world's oil consumption is used for food production and transport. In the United States, on average, fruits and vegetables travel approximately 1,500 miles before reaching your dinner table. Along with the transportation of the produce, each product needs to be packed, stored, and then shipped those 1,500 miles to the store—all of which use energy and gas for transportation. The Natural Resources Defense Council estimated that in California, "the smog-forming emissions from importing fruits and vegetables are equivalent to the annual emissions from 1.5 million cars."

Buying locally grown produce reduces the carbon footprint as less energy is required for shipping. There are other benefits to locally grown food too. Because the produce doesn't travel far, it doesn't have to be picked early, allowing farmers to pick at the peak of freshness.

Through events such as farmers markets, local farmers are given a communal space to sell their produce directly to consumers. This also gives consumers the opportunity to ask the farmer if any chemicals were used in the growing of the food. Agriculture's increasing dependence on pesticides, fertilizers, and hormones poses a great danger to human health and the environment. By buying directly from farmers, consumers not only support the local economy, they also protect their health by knowing exactly what they are eating. Also, local farmers are more likely to spend their money in the community, continuing the cycle for a healthy local economy.

Perhaps even more important than where you buy your food is what you buy. Making one easy switch could dramatically reduce your carbon footprint: consuming less red meat and dairy. Cows are massive contributors to greenhouse gases. It's energy intensive to raise cows, but their flatulence and manure emit methane, which is about twenty-five times more potent as a greenhouse gas than carbon dioxide. Hooved animals are responsible for 50% more pollution than all of the transportation system's production of carbon dioxide combined.

So, be conscious about what you eat. Many cooking blogs promote "meatless Mondays" which is a good habit to get into. Plan your meals around what is in season—sticking to produce that is available locally. It also gives you an opportunity to have a good variety of produce throughout the year!

—Emily Abrams

EAT SMART. YOUR FOOD CHOICES AFFECT THE CLIMATE.

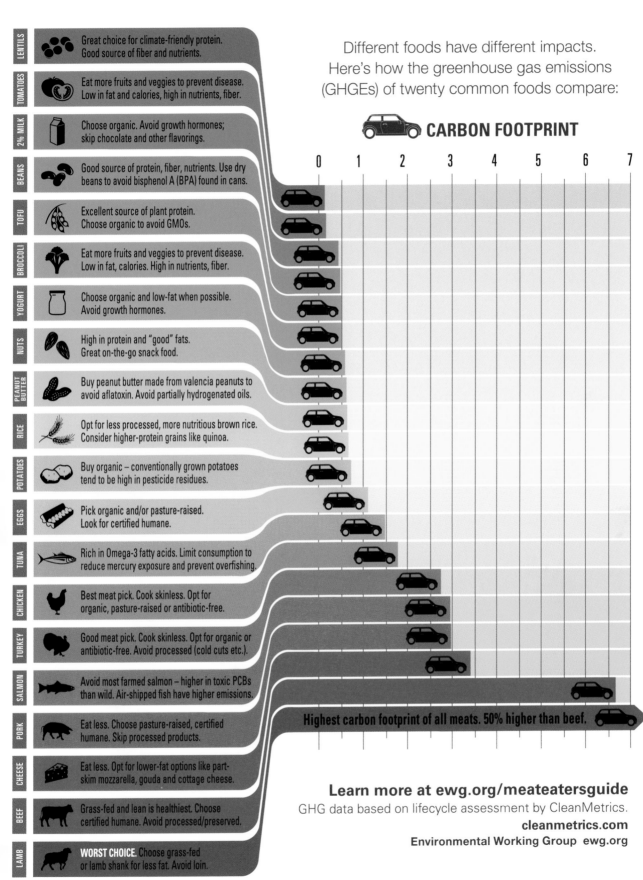

Different foods have different impacts. Here's how the greenhouse gas emissions (GHGEs) of twenty common foods compare:

CARBON FOOTPRINT

LENTILS	Great choice for climate-friendly protein. Good source of fiber and nutrients.
TOMATOES	Eat more fruits and veggies to prevent disease. Low in fat and calories, high in nutrients, fiber.
2% MILK	Choose organic. Avoid growth hormones; skip chocolate and other flavorings.
BEANS	Good source of protein, fiber, nutrients. Use dry beans to avoid bisphenol A (BPA) found in cans.
TOFU	Excellent source of plant protein. Choose organic to avoid GMOs.
BROCCOLI	Eat more fruits and veggies to prevent disease. Low in fat, calories. High in nutrients, fiber.
YOGURT	Choose organic and low-fat when possible. Avoid growth hormones.
NUTS	High in protein and "good" fats. Great on-the-go snack food.
PEANUT BUTTER	Buy peanut butter made from valencia peanuts to avoid aflatoxin. Avoid partially hydrogenated oils.
RICE	Opt for less processed, more nutritious brown rice. Consider higher-protein grains like quinoa.
POTATOES	Buy organic – conventionally grown potatoes tend to be high in pesticide residues.
EGGS	Pick organic and/or pasture-raised. Look for certified humane.
TUNA	Rich in Omega-3 fatty acids. Limit consumption to reduce mercury exposure and prevent overfishing.
CHICKEN	Best meat pick. Cook skinless. Opt for organic, pasture-raised or antibiotic-free.
TURKEY	Good meat pick. Cook skinless. Opt for organic or antibiotic-free. Avoid processed (cold cuts etc.).
SALMON	Avoid most farmed salmon – higher in toxic PCBs than wild. Air-shipped fish have higher emissions.
PORK	Eat less. Choose pasture-raised, certified humane. Skip processed products.
CHEESE	Eat less. Opt for lower-fat options like part-skim mozzarella, gouda and cottage cheese.
BEEF	Grass-fed and lean is healthiest. Choose certified humane. Avoid processed/preserved.
LAMB	WORST CHOICE. Choose grass-fed or lamb shank for less fat. Avoid loin.

Highest carbon footprint of all meats. 50% higher than beef.

Learn more at ewg.org/meateatersguide
GHG data based on lifecycle assessment by CleanMetrics.
cleanmetrics.com
Environmental Working Group ewg.org

zesty fish cakes

Rich Vellante, executive chef, Legal Sea Foods
Boston, MA

¾ cup flaked cooked fish
   (preferably pollock)
⅓ cup crushed saltine crackers
   (about 8)
⅛ cup minced fresh basil
⅛ cup minced fresh parsley
   Cayenne pepper
⅔ cup fresh mashed potato
   (about 1 medium)
2 tablespoons sour cream or yogurt
1 large egg
1 teaspoon bottled horseradish
   Salt
   Freshly milled black pepper
   Panko (Japanese bread crumbs)
   Grape seed oil, olive oil, or butter

Global warming has increased the Atlantic Ocean's water temperatures, forcing some indigenous fish species to migrate to colder waters. Legal Sea Foods serves only seafood of unparalleled freshness and quality that is also seasonal, safe, and sustainable. In fact, we've operated with a commitment to sustainability for over three decades. The recipe I'm sharing is a classic and can be made with virtually any leftover fish with a medium-soft texture. The fish you'll find available at your market are within National Oceanic and Atmospheric Administration's (NOAA's) guidelines and, as such, are considered sustainable species by the federal government. But try pollock, which is a local and underutilized species that lends itself well to this particular preparation. Bon appétit!

Combine the fish, crackers, herbs, a pinch of cayenne pepper, the potato, sour cream, egg, and horseradish in a medium bowl. Season with salt and pepper to taste. Divide the fish mixture into cakes about 2 inches in diameter. Place the Panko in a bowl and dip each cake into it to coat lightly.

Pour oil into a large skillet to a depth of ¼ inch. Heat over medium to medium-high heat. Cook the fish cakes on both sides until heated through and the bread crumbs are browned, about 6 minutes. Drain thoroughly on paper towels before serving. Makes 6 fish cakes.

entrees

salmon wrapped in fig leaves with kale

Michael Pollan, professor of journalism, author of _The Omnivore's Dilemma_
Berkeley, CA

4   pieces (3 to 4 ounces each)
       boneless, skinless salmon
     Olive oil
     Course salt and freshly ground
       pepper
4   fig leaves
½   pound kale, torn into small pieces

This dish was inspired by Chez Panisse, which serves something similar. If you don't have a fig tree, go to a nursery and "prune" a couple leaves. Use wild salmon from Alaska or Loch Duart, sustainably farmed salmon from Scotland.

Preheat oven to 350 degrees.

Drizzle salmon with olive oil and season with salt and pepper. Wrap each piece of salmon in a fig leaf and place on a baking sheet. Transfer to oven and bake until cooked through, 10 to 12 minutes. Set aside and keep warm.

Place olive oil in a spray bottle and spray kale with olive oil; season with salt and pepper. Place kale on a baking sheet and transfer to oven. Bake until kale is crispy, about 8 minutes. Divide kale evenly between four plates. Unwrap salmon and serve immediately on fig leaves, atop the kale.

I like to say, "pay more, eat less." There's no escaping the fact that better food—whether measured by taste or nutritional quality (which often correspond)—costs more, usually because it has been grown with more care and less intensively. Not everyone can afford to eat high-quality food in America, and that is shameful; however, those of us who can, should. Doing so benefits not only your health (by, among other things, reducing your exposure to pesticides and pharmaceuticals), but also the health of the people who grow the foods as well as the people who live downstream and downwind of the farms where it is grown.

So while it would have been much simpler to say "eat organic," instead I suggest eating well-grown food from healthy soils. It is true that food certified organic is usually well grown in relatively healthy soils—soils that have been nourished by organic matter rather than synthetic fertilizers. Yet there are exceptional farmers and ranchers in America who for one reason or another are not certified organic and the food they grow should not be overlooked. Organic is important, but it's not the last word on how to grow food well.

I think eating vegetables and fruit is so important that I buy them even when they're not organic—and even when they're not fresh. There's nothing wrong with frozen vegetables, and they're usually a bargain. Some canned vegetables are a great deal, too, though they often have too much salt. The key thing? Eat plants (including whole grains), animals, and fungi as lightly processed as you can find them at the prices you can afford.

—Michael Pollan

spring lamb shepherd's pie

Richard Branson, founder of Virgin Group
London, England

2¼ pounds boneless shoulder of lamb
2 tablespoons flour
Sea salt
Pepper, freshly ground
Olive oil
1 red onion, peeled and roughly chopped
2 sticks of celery, trimmed and roughly chopped
1 carrot, peeled and roughly chopped
1¾ ounces pancetta, roughly chopped
2 cloves of garlic, finely chopped
Rosemary, small bunch with leaves picked
1 14-ounce can of plum tomatoes, chopped
9 ounces lamb or vegetable stock
2¼ pounds Desirée potatoes
7 ounces milk
2 tablespoons butter

On Food Revolution Day, I'll be cooking up my favorite dish, the trusty shepherd's pie. This is the recipe I follow, it's delicious, and I hope you enjoy it.

Preheat the oven to 375° F. Trim any large bits of fat off the lamb then cut the meat into chunks and put small batches into the food processor until minced roughly. Place the mince in a bowl, then add the flour and seasoning and toss until evenly coated.
Heat a large pan, then add a small puddle of olive oil and lamb mince. Fry until browned. Add the onion, celery, carrot, pancetta, and garlic to the pan, and throw in a large pinch of rosemary leaves and the tomatoes. Pour in the stock and stir well so the mixture doesn't stick to the bottom of the pan. Leave in the same pan or transfer to an ovenproof dish, cover, and bake in the oven for an hour.

Peel the potatoes, boil them in salted water until cooked through, then drain well. Heat the milk gently then pour over the potatoes. Add a knob of butter and mash until smooth.

Melt the remaining butter in a frying pan. When it starts to bubble, throw in the rosemary and fry until crisp. Drain, and add the rosemary to the mashed potatoes with salt and freshly ground black pepper.

Remove the lamb from the oven. Spoon the potato mixture over the lamb and return to a 400°F oven and bake for about 20 minutes or until bubbling and crispy brown.

vegetarian chili

Jayni & Chevy Chase
Bedford Corners, NY

3 25 ounce cans of organic beans—
   kidney, black, and pinto
1 red pepper (red has the most
   nutrients so sometimes we use
   more red than green or yellow)
1 yellow pepper
1 green pepper
1 large yellow onion
8-10 cloves garlic
2-3 cups sliced mushrooms (remember
   they shrink way down when
   cooked)
2 tablespoons cumin (or more! We
   love cumin!)
2 tablespoons oregano
1 teaspoon coriander
1 teaspoon ground allspice
1 teaspoon ground cloves
1 tablespoon salt

This is our favorite vegetarian meal. It provides plant protein and so will fill you up and give you all the nutrients you need from a healthy meal. We don't need to have animal protein in our diets to grow strong and be healthy. Think about elephants—they're strictly vegetarian, and they're the largest, strongest mammals on land!

Add cornbread to the meal, and this is dinner. I keep small loaves or sometimes muffins of cornbread in the freezer—they freeze really well and defrost quickly

Pour the beans into a large colander and let drain.

Chop peppers and sauté in a large sauté pan. Chop onion and add once the peppers are starting to soften.

Mince 6 of the garlic cloves and add to pepper mixture in sauté pan.

Add the mushrooms.

Add all the spices. Stir well while cooking for about 2 minutes.

Add the beans, folding them into the vegetables.

Mince the rest of the garlic cloves and fold into ingredients in pan. Now taste. You may find you want to add more salt or cumin or whatever suits your taste buds!

Chevy calls himself "The Egg Man." He loves eggs. It's a really good day when he eats 4 eggs cooked in olive oil, over-medium (whites cooked and yolk runny), each one on a slice of ham on a toasted English muffin. Several years ago we learned that eating eggs can lead to high cholesterol. This was at first very bad news for Chevy, but then we learned this isn't necessarily true. We learned a fact that makes perfect sense—what the chicken has eaten determines whether the egg provides healthy nutrients or not. Chickens are meant to eat all kinds of things—a variety of vegetation, grass, insects (especially worms that have fed on decaying plants), and grains. Unfortunately, factory farm raised chickens are fed only chicken feed—no fresh vegetables, green grass, or worms.

We live on 10 acres and have owned two horses since 1996, so why not build a chicken coop and get some chickens?! We feed them lots of fresh veggies and worms, and we mix flax seeds into their feed. The eggs they provide us have deeply colored yolks and they taste much better. And, more important, we're getting nutrients from eating our own chicken eggs that will contribute to our good health. Best of all, Chevy's cholesterol continues to be a healthy balance of the "good" and the "bad."

—Jayni Chase

turkey breakfast sausage with Dr. Hyman's chinese eggs & seasoned greens

Mark Hyman, MD, author, founder of the UltraWellness Center Lenox, MA

Sausage

- 1 pound ground turkey breast
- ¼ cup finely diced apple, such as gala or red delicious
- 2 tablespoons finely minced red onion
- 2 tablespoons finely minced fresh sage
- ½ teaspoon finely minced fresh thyme
- 3 tablespoons extra-virgin olive oil
- ½ teaspoon sea salt
- ½ teaspoon freshly ground black pepper

Eggs

- 12 cloves garlic
- 6 whole omega-3 eggs
- 3 tablespoons extra-virgin olive oil
- 1 16-ounce can whole or chopped plum tomatoes with juice
- 1 teaspoon toasted sesame oil
- 1 tablespoon reduced-sodium, wheat-free tamari
- 1 teaspoon Worcestershire sauce
- 1 cup cooked brown rice
- 6 cups spinach, steamed

This flavorful breakfast sausage with sage and apple is a delicious, healthy alternative to store-bought sausage. It pairs nicely with the Chinese eggs, which are a tasty variant.

Sausage

In a large bowl, gently mix together the ground turkey, apple, onion, sage, thyme, 1 tablespoon of the extra-virgin olive oil, salt, and pepper. Form the mixture into eight 4-inch patties, each about ½-inch thick.

Heat the remaining 2 tablespoons of extra-virgin olive oil in a nonstick skillet over medium heat. Cook the patties for 3–4 minutes on each side, until firm to the touch.

Eggs

Chop garlic coarsely. Beat eggs with a whisk. Heat extra-virgin olive oil in a 12-inch nonstick sauté pan or wok. Add garlic and cook for 1 minute. Add eggs and let them cook undisturbed until eggs are no longer liquid, and then flip over and cook on the other side. When cooked through, use a spatula to cut eggs into 1- to 2-inch pieces. Add chopped tomatoes and juice to the eggs. Add sesame oil, tamari, and Worcestershire sauce. Simmer for 10 minutes. Serve over brown rice with some steamed spinach.

One hundred years ago, all we ate was local, organic food—grass fed, real, whole food. There were no fast-food restaurants, there was no junk food, there was no frozen food—there was just what your mother or grandmother made. Most meals were eaten at home. Now one in five breakfasts is from McDonald's, and 50 percent of meals are eaten outside the home.

Ultimately, there is no confusion about what constitutes good nutrition, despite the "conflicting" scientific studies and media reports designed to confound rather than enlighten. If we were to gather the world's top nutrition scientists and experts, there would be very little debate about the essential properties of good nutrition. Unfortunately, most doctors are nutritionally illiterate. And worse, they don't know how to use the most powerful medicine available to them: food.

Common sense and scientific research lead us to the conclusion that, if we want healthy bodies, we must put the right raw materials in them: real, whole, local, fresh, unadulterated, unprocessed, and chemical-, hormone-, and antibiotic-free food. There should be no room in our diets for foreign molecules such as trans fats and high-fructose corn syrup or for industrially developed, processed food that interferes with our biology at every level.

Broccoli, peaches, almonds, kidney beans, and other whole foods don't need a food ingredient label or bar code, but for some reason, these foods—the foods we co-evolved with over millennia—had to be "improved" by food science. As a result, the processed food industry and industrial agriculture have changed our diet, decade by decade, not by accident but by intention.

We need to resize our thinking when it comes to eating plants versus animals. And we need to reassess completely our perception of processed foods. Animal foods, if eaten at all, should be a condiment, not the center of the meal. Processed foods, typically, shouldn't be eaten. If it comes out of a package or a can, it isn't real food.

The sustainability of our planet, our health, and our food supply are inextricably linked. The ecology of eating—the importance of what you put on your fork—has never been more critical to our survival as a nation or as a species. The earth will survive our self-destruction. But we may not.

That is why I believe the most important and the most powerful tool you have to change your health and the world is your fork. Imagine an experiment—let's call it a celebration, a Global Eat-In. Imagine if we call upon the people of the world to join together and celebrate food for one day. For one day, we all eat breakfast and dinner at home with our family members or friends. For one day, we will all eat only real, whole, fresh food. Imagine for a moment the power of the fork to change the world.

— Mark Hyman, MD, author, founder of the UltraWellness Center

ikarian stew

**Dan Buettner, author of *The Blue Zones & National Geographic*
explorer**
Minneapolis, MN

½ pound black eyed peas
½ cup extra-virgin olive oil
1 large red onion, finely chopped
2 garlic cloves, finely chopped
1 large, firm ripe tomato, finely
    chopped
2 teaspoons tomato paste, diluted in
    ¼ cup water
2 bay leaves
    Salt to taste
1 bunch wild fennel
1 fennel bulb, finely chopped
1 bunch dill, finely chopped

Rinse the black eyed peas in a colander.

Heat half the olive oil over medium heat and cook the onion and garlic, stirring occasionally, until soft, about 12 minutes.

Add the black eyed peas and toss to coat in the oil.

Add the tomato, tomato paste and enough water to cover the beans by about an inch. Add the bay leaves. Bring to a boil, reduce heat and simmer until the black eyed peas are about half way cooked. (Check after 40 minutes, but it may take over an hour. You don't want stones and you don't want mush. You can also cook this ahead of time and reheat.)

Season with salt. Add the wild fennel. (If wild fennel is unavailable, cook the chopped fennel bulb with the onion and garlic, then add the dill in place of the wild fennel.)

Continue cooking until the black eyed peas are tender. Remove bay leaves, pour in remaining raw olive oil, and serve.

buttermilk chicken

Ken Oringer, James Beard Award winner, chef/proprietor

Mushrooms
- 1 tablespoon olive oil
- 1 pound wild mushrooms
- 2 cloves garlic, chopped
- 1 cup white wine
- 1 cup chicken stock
- 1 tablespoon soy sauce
- 1/4 cup chives, chopped
- 1 cup artichoke hearts
- 1/4 teaspoon lemon juice
- 2 tablespoon butter
- Salt and pepper

Chicken
- 4 chicken breasts, boneless
- 2 cups buttermilk
- 4 sprigs thyme
- 4 cloves garlic, crushed
- Salt and pepper
- 4 large Ziploc bags

To make mushrooms

In a sauté pan, heat olive oil and add mushrooms, sautéing until golden brown. Add garlic and sauté for one minute more.

Add all remaining ingredients and cook until reduced by two-thirds and sauce slightly thickens. Season to taste.

To make chicken

Preheat oven to 350°F. Carefully remove skin from chicken breasts. Place skin on a cookie sheet, season with salt and pepper, and bake until golden brown and crispy. Reserve.

In a Ziploc bag, combine one chicken breast and 1/2 cup buttermilk, 1 garlic clove, and 1 sprig of thyme. Season with salt and pepper. Repeat for remaining 3 chicken breasts.

In a sauce pot filled with simmering water at approximately 149°F, cook chicken in bags for approximately 30 minutes. Remove from bags.

To serve, place some mushrooms on a plate and layer a chicken breast on top. Add more mushrooms atop the chicken and finish with a crispy piece of skin. Makes 4 servings.

Composting is nature's recycling. Why throw your organic waste into the landfill or down the disposal, when you can use all those nutrients to fertilize your garden? Composting is not only for people with acres of land or large gardens—home composting bins are available for city dwellers as well.

rushing waters trout, roasted apples, bacon, grilled lettuce

Paul Virant, chef/proprietor of Vie and Perennial Virant restaurants Chicago, IL

1 medium head romaine, washed and split in half
1 tablespoon olive oil
  Salt and pepper
1 lemon, zested and halved
3 tablespoons grape seed oil
2 4- to 5-oz. rainbow trout fillets (skin-on, pin bones removed)
1 tablespoon butter
2 ounces bacon, diced
1 Honeycrisp apple, peeled, cored, and diced
2 sprigs thyme
1 shallot, sliced

Brush the cut side of the romaine with olive oil. Season with salt and pepper.

Grill on a hot grill for about 2 minutes. Squeeze half a lemon atop to finish.

Remove from grill and place onto a serving platter.

Preheat grape seed oil in a heavy-bottom sauté pan.

Season the fish and sear, skin side down, for about 2 minutes, until the skin is crisp.

Add the butter. Tilt the pan to baste the fish with the butter for about 30 seconds.

Flip the fish and cook a few seconds more. Place fish onto the platter over the romaine.

Degrease the pan, then add the bacon and cook until almost crisp.

Add the apple and thyme; roast about a minute.

Add the shallot. Season with salt and pepper. Add the lemon zest and squeeze the other lemon half.

Spoon mixture over the trout and serve. Makes 2 servings.

Food is life and the environment gives us life.

At my restaurants we strive to source our products from people who care about our world. The trout comes from 56 ponds fed with crystal-clear artesian spring water from a farm in the rolling hills of Wisconsin. The chemical-free trout are fed a premium diet of non-animal by-product feed. This is an example of how we practice sustainability. As I look to the future of food, sourcing locally from conscientious producers will continue to become important to minimize environmental destruction.

—Paul Virant, executive chef, Vie and Perennial Virant restaurants

food

fish stew

Michael Oppenheimer, professor of geosciences, Princeton University
Princeton, NJ

1 large onion, chopped
2 sweet red peppers, chopped
1 head fennel, chopped
 Olive oil
3 pounds mussels, in shell
1 dozen cherrystone (or soft shell) clams, in shell
1 cup wine
1 dozen shrimp, in shell or peeled
1 pound fish, filleted and diced into 1-inch cubes
 Tomato paste
 Turmeric or curry powder
 Chili powder

This dish is best prepared from local seafood. Check the site seafood.edf.org to confirm its sustainability rating. The beauty of the recipe is that the individual fish ingredients are largely fungible: Your favorite species are not always available fresh or rated high in sustainability, but you can usually switch to something similar that satisfies both criteria. For example, we generally use clams we dig ourselves in Rhode Island during the summer. Cod is a good fish to use but sustainable cod in the eastern U.S. may be hard to find. We suggest trying tilapia or another meaty white-fleshed fish for which sustainable varieties are more easily found. We sometimes use striped bass caught by local sport fishers, but U.S. catfish, Barramundi, or farmed striped bass would also do, according to the EDF list. Fennel, red pepper, and onion can all be grown locally in southern New England, where we spend our summers.

Sauté the onion, red peppers, and fennel in olive oil. Transfer the sautéed mixture to a soup pot and add the mussels, clams, and wine (to taste, substituting some water if desired).

Bring to a low boil and simmer on a low flame until mussels and clams open and release their liquid. (Discard any shellfish that do not open.)

Add shrimp and simmer an additional 5 minutes, then add fish and simmer another 5 minutes. Add tomato paste and spices to taste. Turn off flame and let the stew sit for 30 minutes before serving.

ENVIRONMENTAL DEFENSE FUND'S SEAFOOD SELECTOR
Fish choices that are good for you, and for the oceans

ECO-FRIENDLY/BEST CHOICES

ABALONE (FARMED)
ALASKA COD (LONGLINE)
  ALBACORE (U.S., CANADA)
ARCTIC CHAR (FARMED)
ATLANTIC MACKEREL (CANADA)
ATLANTIC POLLOCK
  BARRAMUNDI (U.S.)
BAY SCALLOPS (FARMED)
  BLACK SEA BASS (TRAP-CAUGHT)
BLUE MUSSEL
CATFISH (U.S.)
CRAWFISH (U.S.)
DUNGENESS CRAB
  EASTERN OR AMERICAN OYSTER
LONGFIN SQUID (U.S.)
  MAHIMAHI (U.S. TROLL/POLE)
MEDITERRANEAN MUSSEL
  PACIFIC HALIBUT (ALASKA AND
  CANADA)
  PACIFIC LITTLENECK (FARMED)
PACIFIC OYSTER
PACIFIC SARDINES (U.S. & CANADA)
  PINK SHRIMP (OREGON)
RAINBOW TROUT (FARMED)
SABLEFISH/BLACK COD (ALASKA,
CANADA)
SALMON (CANNED)
  SNOW CRAB (US)
SOFTSHELL CLAM
SPINY LOBSTER
 STRIPED BASS (FARMED)
STRIPED MULLET
  TILAPIA (ECUADOR)
TILAPIA (U.S.)
  U.S. HADDOCK (HOOK AND LINE)
  WEATHERVANE SCALLOP
WILD ALASKAN SALMON
WRECKFISH
YELLOW PERCH (LAKE ERIE)
YELLOWFIN (U.S. ATLANTIC TROLL/
POLE)

ECO-FRIENDLY/WORST CHOICES

ALBACORE (IMPORTED, LONGLINE)
ATLANTIC HALIBUT
ATLANTIC OR FARMED SALMON
ATLANTIC POLLOCK (ICELAND/DANISH
SEINE, TRAWL)
ATLANTIC STURGEON
BELUGA STURGEON (WILD, IMPORTED)
BLACK SEA BASS (TRAWL-CAUGHT)
BLACKFIN (ATLANTIC LONGLINE/PURSE
SEINE)
BLUE KING CRAB (IMPORTED)
BLUE MARLIN (IMPORTED)
BLUE SHRIMP
BLUEFIN
  CALIFORNIA HALIBUT (SET GILLNET)
  CARIBBEAN SPINY LOBSTER
(IMPORTED)
CHINESE WHITE SHRIMP
CRAWFISH (IMPORTED)
  FRESHWATER EEL
GIANT TIGER PRAWN
GROUPER (IMPORTED)
IMPORTED SNAPPER
LAKE STURGEON (WILD, IMPORTED)
LONGFIN MAKO
MAHIMAHI (IMPORTED, LONGLINE)
OCTOPUS
ORANGE ROUGHY
RED KING CRAB (IMPORTED)
RUSSIAN STURGEON
SHRIMP AND PRAWNS (IMPORTED)
SKATE
SOUTHERN FLOUNDER
STRIPED MARLIN
STURGEON (WILD, IMPORTED)
SWORDFISH (IMPORTED)
TRAWL)
YELLOWTAIL (FARMED, AUSTRALIA,
JAPAN)

For more information, go to EDF.org

roasted lemon sole

Babylon Restaurant
London, England

4   whole lemon soles, cleaned by your
    fish monger
1   teaspoon butter (softened)
    Salt and pepper
16 Jersey Royal baby potatoes
⅓ cup extra-virgin olive oil
4   salted anchovy fillets
1.4 ounces samphire (also known as
    "sea asparagus")
8   cherry tomatoes, halved
1¾ ounces toasted pine nuts
1   red pepper, finely diced
    Fresh chopped herbs (either dill
    or chervil)
1   lemon

Lay the lemon sole onto a baking sheet and brush with soft butter. Season with salt and pepper (to taste). Place in a 350°F oven for approximately 12-15 minutes.

Place potatoes in a pan of lightly salted water. Bring to a boil and then simmer until tender for about 10 minutes before draining.

Place the olive oil in a saucepan and warm gently on low heat with the anchovy fillets until they have broken down.

Blanch the samphire in boiling water for 10 seconds and drain.

Mix the samphire, cherry tomatoes, pine nuts, red pepper, and fresh herbs into the anchovy sauce and warm through on low heat. Place the sole fillets onto a serving plate and dress with the anchovy sauce.

Serve with the boiled Jersey Royal potatoes and a wedge of lemon. Makes 4 servings.

"This risotto made with **beets has a beautiful magenta** color when finished, which is a nice surprise for guests."

—John Podesta

risotto alla barbabietola (beet risotto)

John Podesta, Chair of the Center for American Progress Washington, D.C.

3 medium red beets
1 medium onion, chopped
  Olive oil
  Salt
  Fresh black pepper
2 cups chicken (or vegetable) stock plus 2 cups water
1½ cups Arborio rice
1 cup dry white wine
1 cup grated Parmesan cheese
2 tablespoons chopped fresh dill

Peel the beets and grate them using the grating blade on a food processor or the large holes on a hand grater.

Using a 4-6-quart flat-bottomed pot, sauté onion in 1 tablespoon olive oil until golden.

Add the beets, a pinch of salt, and several grinds of pepper. Cover and cook on medium to medium-low heat until beets soften (approximately 10 minutes); stir occasionally, making sure the beets don't stick.

In another pot, bring stock and water to a low simmer; this will be added a little at a time to the rice.

When the beets are softened and partially cooked, add the rice and 1 tablespoon olive oil. Stir for a minute or two until the rice is well coated.

Add the wine and stir until liquid is completely evaporated.

Add ½ cup of hot broth and stir into rice; when the liquid is absorbed, add another ½ cup and stir. Keep repeating until most of the liquid is absorbed. If rice begins to stick on the bottom, add some broth and scrape it up with a wooden spoon.

The rice is done when it is al dente, firm to the bite, creamy, neither chalky (underdone) nor gluey (overdone). The liquid is an approximation. You need to adjust liquid—a little more or a little less—accordingly.

When rice is done, remove from the heat. Add a heaping ½ cup of Parmesan and stir into the rice. Serve the remaining Parmesan on the side at the table.

Serve the rice in bowls with a good pinch of dill sprinkled on top. Makes 6 servings.

grilled skuna bay salmon with rainbow chard & golden beet puree

Michael Kornick, chef/proprietor of MK Restaurant
Chicago, IL

Rainbow Chard
- 2 tablespoons grape seed oil
- 1/2 cup diced pancetta
- 1/4 cup sliced garlic
- 1 bunch rainbow chard, leaves only and cleaned of stems
- 1/2 cup cleaned and diced chard stems

Golden Beet Puree:
- 1 large golden beet, roasted, peeled, and diced
- 1/3 cup champagne vinegar
  Water, as needed
- 1/2 cup grape seed oil
  Salt and pepper to taste

Skuna Bay Salmon
- 4 6 ounce Skuna Bay Salmon fillets, skinless (2 inch thick)
  Salt and pepper to taste
- 2 tablespoons grape seed oil
- 1 lemon, cut into wedges

For the Rainbow Chard:
Heat grape seed oil and render pancetta slowly. Add sliced garlic; sweat but do not brown.

Add chard stems and stir. Add chard leaves and cook down. Do not cover and do not braise. Total cooking time should be 5 to 8 minutes.

For the Golden Beet Puree:
Place beet in blender with champagne vinegar and blend. Add water only if needed to enable blending. Stir in grape seed oil, and season to taste.

For the Skuna Bay Salmon:
Season salmon fillets with the salt and pepper. Gently rub oil on salmon fillets to prevent them from sticking to grill grates.

Place fillets on hot grill. Flip after 2 1/2 minutes and continue cooking for another 2 1/2 minutes for a medium-rare piece of fish. Finish with a squeeze of lemon.

To plate:
In a small saucepan gently warm the beet puree just to room temperature and place a spoonful in the middle of each plate.

Place the heated rainbow chard on top of the puree and then the fish on top of the chard. Feel free to garnish with a fresh salad of garden greens drizzled lightly with aged balsamic vinegar.

At MK our goal is to source locally in order to create the smallest carbon footprint possible. We begin this approach by creating strong relationships with vendors that share the same goal. This recipe was created after visiting Vancouver Island and witnessing the tireless passion that is demonstrated through the Skuna Bay process. The common thread shared between our partners is a focus on quality while maintaining the delicate balance of sustainability. We are very proud to have the opportunity to work with committed farmers on both the land and sea. Our customers recognize this effort through their loyal support of not just MK and its staff but the greater task at hand.

—Michael Kornick

artichoke risotto

Amy Kellogg, Fox News correspondent
London, England

6 artichokes
Olive oil
Fresh parsley, chopped
Garlic
Salt
Pepper
10 handfuls of risotto rice
White wine
Vegetable broth
  (no more than 3 cups)
Butter or oil
Parmesan cheese

You can follow the same steps of this recipe using zucchini, porcini mushrooms, or asparagus—whatever is seasonal, local, and therefore won't require serious transportation!

This dish is delicious but it can also help to "not" cook the planet because you should use local, seasonal vegetables that don't need to travel by plane to get to your kitchen.

So if you are in California, artichokes might be your magic ingredient. In New Jersey, you might embrace the asparagus version.

Artichokes should be young and fresh—if they have hair, "the choke"—they won't be any good for this dish, according to my sources in Italy!

Take off the hardest leaves of the artichokes so you just have soft leaves and hearts left. Cut up artichokes and fry them with the olive oil, chopped parsley, garlic (you can fry garlic whole and then remove it so flavor remains but the garlic is gone), salt, and pepper for a few minutes.

Add enough water so mix is just covered. and let it simmer until water is absorbed.

In another pan, heat up some olive oil and stir rice in with a wooden spoon.

Add white wine and stir until it evaporates. Then add some of the vegetable sauce, stirring until it is absorbed. Keep adding a bit of broth, then a bit more, letting the rice absorb it as you go.

When it's ready, add a little butter or oil and a handful of Parmesan cheese.

We know what rising carbon pollution is doing to our planet. We have seen the devastation from superstorms and drought with our own eyes. The potential for disaster is terrifying, but we cannot be immobilized. The opportunity to build something better can inspire us to action.

I grew up in rural west Tennessee. People there have been eating pork ribs for generations. That is why I love my Summertime Ribs so much. It is true to where I came from—but it is not only delicious, it is organic and eco-friendly!

It is possible to be both prosperous AND green. We can innovate new approaches while holding on to the best of the old. We can build an economy where everyone who wants a job can get one, without cooking the planet we depend on to survive. We just need to muster the will to act.

It is the 21st century. If you can read this book, you can launch a movement. The idea that will change the whole game and save our planet is out there right now. It just needs more champions. Creativity does not come from lobbyists. Change does not come from Washington, D.C. The tired old playbook is failing. It is time to cook up something new.

—Van Jones

chang

summertime ribs with heirloom tomato, corn & basil bread salad

Van Jones, host of CNN's *Crossfire*, former advisor to
President Barack Obama
Los Angeles, CA

Summertime Ribs
- ½ teaspoon salt
- 1 tablespoon sugar
- ½ tablespoon ground cumin
- ½ tablespoon freshly ground pepper
- ½ tablespoon chili powder
- 1 tablespoon paprika
- ½ teaspoon cinnamon
- 4 pounds organic, pasture-raised pork spareribs

Heirloom Tomato, Corn & Basil Bread Salad
- ¼ pound crusty bread, such as ciabatta
- 4 tablespoons extra-virgin olive oil
  Kosher salt (to taste)
  Freshly ground black pepper (to taste)
- 2 ears of corn, husks removed
- 1½ tablespoons white balsamic vinegar
- ¼ cup finely chopped fresh basil
- ¾ pound assorted heirloom tomatoes, cored and cut into ½-inch pieces
- ¼ pound small heirloom cherry tomatoes, cut in half
- 1 large ball of fresh mozzarella, cut into ½-inch pieces

Summertime Ribs

Preheat oven to 300°F.

Mix the salt, sugar, and all the spices together and rub mixture well into the ribs; place in a roasting pan in single layer.

Bake ribs, pouring off accumulated fat every 30 minutes or so, for about 2 hours, or until the ribs are cooked.

When you are ready to eat, roast the ribs at 500°F for about 10 minutes, or run them under the broiler until nicely browned (watch closely so they don't burn!). Makes 4 to 6 servings.

Heirloom Tomato, Corn & Basil Bread Salad*

Preheat oven to 400°F.

Cut the bread into 1-inch cubes, then toss with 1 tablespoon of the olive oil, adding salt and pepper to taste. Spread on a baking sheet and bake for 8 to 10 minutes, until golden brown and crispy.

Bring a large pot of water to a boil. Add corn and cook for 4 to 5 minutes, or until tender; drain. Let cool completely, then cut kernels off cobs.

*Use seasonal, organic, local ingredients whenever possible!

TWO Restaurant is a farm to fork restaurant that utilizes sustainable ingredients from trusted small Midwestern farmers. We go to great lengths to do everything possible in house: curing and smoking our own meats, homemade pasta, house made sausage, and using the entire animal. We feel that food sourced locally tastes better. For this recipe we use duck eggs for the pasta from a local farmer in Michigan; ducks are more humanely raised than chickens, and the difference is in the bright orange yolks that yield excellent pasta. Duck eggs are available seasonally at farmers markets as well as specialty stores; with a little effort your work will be rewarded. This dish speaks to the big flavors we strive for daily in the kitchen at TWO. Fresh duck egg pasta, homemade duck confit, duck skin cracklins, all sautéed in duck fat. We get our duck legs from Indiana—they travel a shorter distance from pasture to plate thus using less fuel and leaving a smaller carbon footprint. Cooking the duck legs in their own fat not only creates a rich flavor, but also utilizes part of the animal that is traditionally wasted.

duck egg pasta with duck confit

Kevin Cuddihee, chef de cuisine, TWO Restaurant
Chicago, IL

6 duck eggs

4 cups pasta flour

1 tablespoon extra-virgin
   olive oil

2 tablespoons whole milk
   Kosher salt

4 duck leg hind quarters

2 pounds rendered duck fat

¼ cup sugar

1 teaspoon cracked black
   peppercorns

1 bunch thyme

3 bay leaves

4 cloves of garlic

1 bunch of scallions
   Parmesan cheese

Duck Confit

Combine 1 cup of kosher salt with ¼ cup of sugar, 1 teaspoon of freshly cracked black peppercorns, 1 bunch of thyme, 3 bay leaves, and 4 cloves of thinly sliced garlic together in a small bowl. Generously rub the salt mixture on the 4 duck leg hindquarters, place in a non-reactive container, cover, and refrigerate 5 hours or overnight. After duck legs have cured rinse the legs under cold running water and dry with paper towels. Preheat oven to 250 degrees. Place dry duck legs in a small square baking dish in one layer. Melt duck fat over medium heat in a sauce pan. Carefully pour melted duck fat over duck legs so that the legs are submerged. Place duck legs in preheated oven for 4 hours. After 4 hours, carefully remove duck from the oven and allow to cool slightly. With a slotted spoon, remove duck legs and place on a cutting board. Carefully remove the duck skin and place on a lined baking sheet. Remove bones and cartilage, pull duck meat apart, and place in a bowl until ready to serve. Strain duck fat, and reserve for another use.

For Pasta

Note: Pasta dough can be made by hand or in a mixer; however, you should always finish kneading the dough by hand to create the best tasting pasta.

Combine 3 duck eggs and 3 duck egg yolks with 1 tablespoon extra-virgin olive oil, 2 tablespoons whole milk, and 1 pinch of kosher salt. Whisk egg mixture until combined. Take roughly 3 cups of pasta flour and make a mound on a clean counter. Create a well in the flour and pour in egg mixture; with a fork slowly incorporate flour into egg mixture. When your dough is combined enough to form a ball, knead with the palm of your hand for 6-8 minutes or until the dough will not take on any more flour and will spring back when you push on it gently. Wrap the dough in plastic wrap and allow it to rest in the refrigerator for at least 45 minutes.

"I think it's important to know where our food comes from. Relationships with farmers is what sets our food apart from others. Not only does it provide a story to our cuisine but **it increases our appreciation for the ingredients we use daily.**"

—Kevin Cuddihee

Cut pasta dough into 4 equal pieces. On a lightly floured surface, press dough into a rectangle shape. Roll the pasta 10 times, making sure the dough is floured to prevent sticking. After the tenth pass, fold the dough in thirds, and pass 10 more times. Keeping the dough floured, adjust your roller to the next widest setting, and pass the dough 3 times. Continue this with each setting until desired thickness (I prefer the fourth setting). Cut your pasta sheets approximately 10 inches long, then using the fettuccini cutter cut your sheets into noodles. Repeat process for all of your pasta dough. After cutting your pasta, allow it to dry on a pasta drying rack or a sheet tray until you are ready to cook.

Heat oven to 350° F, place pan with duck skins in the oven, and bake for 10-15 minutes or until duck skins are crispy but not burnt. Place on a dry paper towel until ready to serve.

Thinly slice one bunch of scallions on the bias.

Fill a large pot of salted water and bring to a boil.

In a large sauté pan over medium heat, add 1 tablespoon of duck fat. After fat melts add pulled duck meat, scallions, and season with salt and black pepper. When water is at a rolling boil drop in pasta stirring occasionally to prevent sticking; fresh pasta cooks in about two minutes. When pasta floats, taste a noodle for doneness. When the pasta is cooked to your liking drain and toss in sauté pan with duck. Taste again and re-season with salt and black pepper. Serve pasta in a bowl and top with shaved Parmesan cheese and crispy duck skins.

Photo by Kathryn Gamble

fresh ham with 1,000 cloves of garlic

Meredith Brokaw, author of *Big Sky Cooking*
New York City, NY/West Boulder Valley, MT

¼ cup vegetable oil
1 (2 inch) piece of fresh ginger; peeled and grated (1 to 2 tablespoons)
1 tablespoon soy sauce
1 (16-pound) whole fresh ham, scored
3 garlic heads, broken apart, cloves unpeeled
3 tablespoons sherry or applejack brandy
2 cups beef broth (bouillon cubes or canned is fine)
2 tablespoons butter
2 tablespoons all-purpose flour
Kosher salt and freshly ground black pepper

Preheat oven to 300º F.

In a small bowl, combine the oil, ginger, and soy sauce; rub the paste all over the ham. Place the ham on a rack in a large roasting pan. Place 3 or 4 large garlic cloves in the pan and place the pan on the bottom rack in the oven. Roast 5 hours; discard the garlic. Add the remaining unpeeled garlic cloves. Continue roasting until an instant-read thermometer inserted deep into the ham registers 160 degrees, 1 to 2 hours longer.

Transfer the ham to a large platter and let rest for 15 minutes. Reserve the garlic cloves.

To make gravy: Discard all but 1 tablespoon fat from the pan. Place the pan over medium heat and add the sherry or brandy, scraping the brown bits from the bottom of the pan. Stir in the broth and bring to a simmer. With a fork, mash the butter and flour into a paste—a *beurre manie*. Whisk the paste into the gravy; continue whisking until thickened. Season to taste with salt and pepper. Strain the gravy through a fine-mesh sieve and keep warm.

To serve, cut the ham into slices. Serve each portion with some crackling, a few garlic cloves, and a ladle of gravy.

Photo by Emily Abrams

red lentil chili

Sharla & Senator Jon Tester
Big Sandy, Montana

1½ cups organic red lentils
4   cups water
1   packet dry onion soup mix
2   14-ounce cans tomatoes
1   teaspoon chili powder
2   teaspoons cumin

Bring lentils to a boil in the 4 cups water. Add the onion soup mix and simmer for 30 minutes. Add the remaining ingredients and simmer for another 30 minutes. Enjoy!

Q&A

—Emily Abrams

Jon Tester was elected to the U.S. Senate in 2006 from the state of Montana. Prior to serving in the Senate, he worked as an organic farmer growing wheat, barley, lentils, peas, millet, buckwheat, and alfalfa. Senator Tester and his wife, Sharla, continue to operate their farm in Big Sandy, Montana.

Emily: Why do you feel so strongly about organic farming versus conventional methods?

Senator Tester: First off, it works for me. Secondly, I certainly don't have anything against conventional methods and I think that if you can make a living off the land and not impact you neighbor negatively, it can be fine. I am a strong believer in organics because it works for us. I don't think we'd be on the farm if we hadn't made the conversion in the late 1980s. I think there are some health issues that we are able to take advantage of and I think there are some issues about overall sustainability that we are able to take advantage of. Now that doesn't come without its challenges but for the most part we have been able to manage those for the last 25 years.

Emily: What made you get involved in organic farming?

Senator Tester: A couple things—in the mid-1980s we were becoming the smallest [farm] out on the block and we knew that we had to do something that added value to our product or else we weren't going to be able to stay in business. My wife never got along well with seed treat [a pesticide] and we quit that in the early 80s. I didn't get along well with the weeder so we quit that as well. This was just a natural thing, and we then began to buy organic durum wheat and we were told what the standards were and we tried it and it worked. And we were off to the races. But with that said it was a number of things: knowing we had to add value to our crop otherwise we weren't going to be able to stay on the farm; and the fact that we never personally got along well with chemicals.

Emily: How do you see climate change affecting the farmers in Montana today?

Senator Tester: I think what we are seeing is more erratic weather. We always say "If you don't like the weather wait an hour." Boy, that was true in the 60s... it's wild now. I mean, what we are seeing across the country is no happy medium. It's either feast or famine; either you're getting drought or you're getting flooded out. Three years ago, for example, there were areas getting flooded out and the water was as high as the roofs of some houses. The very next year that same area didn't get a drop of water and they couldn't raise crops because they didn't have any water. So I think what we are seeing is very wide swings in weather patterns and that is probably the biggest change in our climate. I personally think that our winters are getting warmer and shorter. There is just no happy medium.

Emily: I read that in Montana, a million acres of trees have been lost from beetle kill. The beetles aren't dying because it's not getting cold enough. What would you say to someone who asked you what they could do to fix the problem? What do you think is the best method?

Senator Tester: I think it is not unlike farming—you have to approach things from many different angles. I think it's the same thing with climate change. We need to look for alternate sources of energy that are affordable. We have to conserve energy that we use. We have to be smarter on the way we manufacture, the way we grow food. The list goes on and on. So, I think you look for every opportunity there is to reduce CO_2 impact and I think that's the best way to do it. It has to be financially sustainable or else people aren't going to do it.

pasta with ham & peas

Middlebury Foods
Middlebury, VT

1 pound of your favorite pasta
2 cups peas
½ pound diced ham
½ stick butter
Salt and pepper

Cut the ham into thin strips or bite-size pieces.

Fill a medium-sized pot with water and boil the water. (Tip: adding two spoonfuls of salt to the water will make the pasta taste much better.) Add the pasta to the water and cook until al dente. Drain the pasta.

Melt the butter in a medium-sized pan over low heat. Add the ham and the peas and turn the heat up to medium. Stir the peas and the ham for two minutes, making sure the butter covers everything.

Add the peas and the ham to the pasta in a bowl.

Optional: sprinkle some black pepper and cheese or salt on top.

Serve!

Middlebury Foods is a self-sustaining, non-profit hunger relief program designed to address the widespread societal issues related to hunger insecurity and nutrition. We have one simple goal: to offer fresh produce and high-quality meats at affordable prices. By cutting out the supermarket and buying from wholesale distributors, we are able to save our customers almost 40%. We source the majority of our food from local Vermont distributors. This allows us to offer extremely fresh and nutritious vegetables, fruits, and meat throughout the year. We package this healthy food and include enough to feed a family of four dinner each night for a week. Because we want everyone to eat healthier while enjoying our products, we include recipes for each customer. We create each recipe personally by combining a number of different ingredients from each box of food. Before including a recipe in our box, we carefully test it to ensure a great taste. The recipes are meant to offer a simple and healthy approach to preparing a tasty meal, and our customers have loved each and every recipe.

fettuccine carbonara with broccolini

Jill Silverman Hough, author of *100 Perfect Pairings Cookbook* series & co-author of *The Clean Plates Cookbook*
Napa, CA

- 1 cup pancetta, cut into ¼-inch cubes (about 4 oz.)
- 12 ounces fettuccine or other favorite pasta
- 3½ cups broccolini (about 1 medium bunch), cut into ¾-inch pieces
- 4 large eggs
- ⅔ cup finely grated Parmesan cheese, plus more for serving
- ⅓ cup finely grated Pecorino cheese, plus more for serving
- 2 cloves garlic, minced
- ½ teaspoon freshly ground black pepper, or more to taste

Pasta carbonara is one of my all-time favorite pastas—because it's so easy to make yet so full of flavor. Hot, just-cooked pasta is tossed with eggs, cheese, and crisped pancetta, making a flavorful, creamy-cheesy sauce. Often, the dish includes peas, but this cold weather version substitutes wintery broccolini.

Nine times out of ten when cooking pasta, I'd say to make the water well salted—1 tablespoon of coarse kosher salt per quart. That's pretty salty, but it really does take that much salt to get enough into the pasta to thoroughly season it. In this dish, there's already a good amount of salt in the pancetta and cheeses. So season the pasta water only half as much.

In a medium skillet over medium-low heat, cook the pancetta, stirring occasionally, until crisp, about 10 minutes. Use a slotted spoon to transfer the pancetta to a large bowl. Set aside to cool.

In a large pot of boiling, mildly salted water, cook the fettuccine according to package directions. Stir in the broccolini 3 minutes before the pasta is al dente.

While the pasta is cooking, add the eggs, cheeses, garlic, and pepper to the pancetta, whisking to combine.

Reserve ½ cup of the pasta-cooking water, then drain. Immediately add the pasta and half of the reserved cooking water to the egg mixture, tossing to combine. Taste and add more pepper and/or cooking water if you like. Serve hot, passing additional cheese at the table.

grilled halibut with herb caper vinaigrette

Debbie MacTavish, gourmet chef, & Craig MacTavish, general manager of Edmonton Oilers, former NHL player and coach Edmonton, Canada

For marinade:
- 1 tablespoon Dijon mustard
- 1 tablespoon lemon juice
- 1 tablespoon chopped tarragon
- 1 teaspoon chopped garlic
- ½ teaspoon lemon zest
- 3 tablespoons olive oil
- Salt and pepper
- 6 6-ounce halibut portions

For vinaigrette:
- 2 tablespoons red wine vinegar
- 1 tablespoon chopped chives
- 1 tablespoon chopped tarragon
- 1 tablespoon capers, rinsed and chopped
- 1 teaspoon grainy Dijon mustard
- ¼ cup olive oil
- Salt and freshly ground black pepper

For vine tomatoes & horseradish fraiche:
- 1 pound Campari tomatoes or cocktail-size tomatoes on the vine
- ½ cup crème fraîche
- 1 tablespoon prepared horseradish

For marinade:
Combine 1 tablespoon mustard, lemon juice, tarragon, garlic, and lemon zest in a small bowl. Whisk in 3 tablespoons olive oil until uniform, and season with salt and pepper to taste. Spread mixture over halibut and allow to stand at room temperature while preparing vinaigrette.

Combine vinegar, chives, tarragon, capers, and 1 teaspoon grainy mustard in a small bowl. Whisk in ¼ cup olive oil and season with salt and pepper to taste. Reserve.

Preheat grill to medium-high heat. Oil the section of grill where you plan to cook fish. Place halibut skin-side up on grill and cook for 5 minutes or until the fish is grill-marked and easy to flip. Cook halibut on skin side for 5 minutes longer or until fish is firm and opaque. Remove from grill. Drizzle fillets with vinaigrette and serve.

For vine tomatoes & horseradish fraiche:
(garnish for the grilled halibut)
Place tomatoes on grill and cook with the lid closed for about 7 minutes or until they are grill-marked and the skin has begun to split. Stir crème fraîche and horseradish together, and either drizzle over vegetables or serve alongside so that guests may help themselves.

balinese grilled chicken

Astrid Haryati, architect, activist, assistant to the Minister of Trade Jakarta, Indonesia

10 garlic cloves, halved
3 fresh long red chiles, halved and seeded
6 small shallots, halved
2 tablespoons chopped fresh ginger
1 teaspoon ground turmeric
¼ cup vegetable oil, plus more for brushing
Salt and freshly ground pepper
1 4-pound chicken, butterflied
4 fresh bay leaves
4 limes, halved

Make sure to harvest at least some of the ingredients from your kitchen window boxes, home garden, or buy them from locally sourced fresh markets.

In a food processor...no, let's not do that. Traditional Indonesian cooks use basic knives to chop, and a mortar and pestle to grind food. Try it, it's easy!

Chop garlic, chiles, shallots, ginger, and turmeric until fine. Add ¼ cup of vegetable oil and grind until fine you've created a paste, then transfer the paste to a small skillet and cook over moderate heat (gas stove, please), stirring, until fragrant and lightly browned, about 5 minutes. Let the paste cool completely and season with salt and pepper.

Set the chicken in a baking dish and rub the paste all over it. Top with bay leaves. Cover and refrigerate for at least four hours or overnight. Stop....no need to do that. Setting them at room temperature for a few hours is perfectly fine. There were no refrigerators when this traditional recipe was invented anyway! Plan your meal in advance so that you do not need to refrigerate anything.

The best choice for cooking this dish is a gas or stovetop grill. Line the grate with a double sheet of heavy-duty aluminum foil, brushed lightly with oil. Transfer the chicken to the foil, skin side up. Cover and grill over moderate heat (350 to 375 degrees) for one hour, or until nearly cooked through. Add the limes to the foil and grill the chicken until the juices run clear when an inner thigh is pierced, about 15 minutes longer. Carve the chicken, transfer to a platter, and serve with the limes.

chicken from Kilimanjaro

Florent Ipananga, Snow Africa Adventures Ltd.
Arusha Tanzania

1 3-pound chicken, cut into 8 pieces
1 tablespoon ginger, minced
1 teaspoon garlic, chopped
½ cup of Marsala wine
4 tablespoons sunflower oil
  Salt
  Pepper

Mix ginger, garlic, and wine, then marinate chicken pieces overnight in the refrigerator.

Coat skillet with roughly ½ tablespoon of oil, then cook chicken in batches until the skin is golden brown and the internal temperature reaches 165 degrees.

Photo by Gabriel Viti

Global warming has affected Mount Kilimanjaro and Tanzania in general. When I remember the first time I climbed Mount Kilimanjaro 14 years ago, the top of the mountain was covered by snow. The snow was hanging all around the mountain. At that time, at the top of Kilimanjaro, it was very cold (up to -35c during the night time). As the temperatures have risen on the mountain due to global warming, there is less snow every year. At the eastern side of the Kibo summit, there is very little snow remaining. On the southern side and western side, there is still snow but it is getting less and less every day.

Mawenzi peak, the second highest peak on Kilimanjaro, also was covered by snow at the time I started climbing the mountain. But nowadays, the snow on the top of Mawenzi is gone due to global warming.

We have very high temperatures now on the mountain during the day time and scientists predict in 30 years, the snow on the top of Kilimanjaro will be gone—which is bad news to us.

The forest around Kilimanjaro is the source of water for the people who are living around Kilimanjaro and Moshi town; the forest is getting less water every day. People are having problems getting water nowadays compared with 5-10 years ago. Tanzania is experiencing drought every year. The Tanzanian government is trying its best to make sure people plant more trees around Kilimanjaro, and in our country as whole, to make sure that carbon dioxide is reduced. But this is not easy and our campaign to plant trees will not solve the problem because it is a global issue.

The world in general must plant trees and use other technologies for sources of energy. If we continue to use fuel, our campaign will mean nothing.

—Florent Ipananga, Arusha, Tanzania

anJaro

Thai chili burger

Andy Lansing, president and CEO of Levy Restaurants
Chicago, IL

Thai Burger Patty:
- 12 ounces ground Niman Ranch pork
- 12 ounces ground Niman Ranch beef
- ¼ cup minced yellow onion
- 1 teaspoon garlic puree
- 1 tablespoon vegetable oil
- 1 teaspoon ginger puree
- 1 teaspoon chile paste
- 1 teaspoon soy sauce
- 1 teaspoon lemon grass puree
- 2 tablespoons minced green onion
- 1 teaspoon Kosher salt
- ½ cup sweet chile sauce (Mae Ploy brand)
- 4 buns

Asian Slaw:
- 1 cup shredded Napa cabbage
- ¼ cup shredded carrots
- ¼ cup julienne snow peas
- 1 tablespoon minced green onion
- ¼ cup chopped cilantro
- 1 ounce rice vinegar
- 1 tablespoon sesame oil

For Asian Slaw:
Mix all of the prepped vegetables in a bowl. Add vinegar and oil just before serving so the slaw stays crisp.

For Thai Burger:
Preheat grill, sauté pan, or cast iron skillet over medium-high heat. Mix burger ingredients (except sweet chile sauce) together and gently form into 4 patties.

Place burger patties on grill for 8 minutes. After 8 minutes, turn burgers over and continue to cook for 5 to 8 minutes longer or until burgers are cooked completely.

While burgers are cooking, grill buns on grill or toast in the oven—whichever you prefer.

Remove burgers from grill and brush each patty with the sweet chile sauce. Place cooked burgers on toasted buns and top with slaw.

linguini with fresh gulf shrimp

Gabriel Viti, executive chef/proprietor of Miramar Bistro Highwood, IL

24 ounces linguini
2 ounces olive oil
2 ounces garlic, raw and chopped
20 pieces shrimp, cut in half
5 plum tomatoes, seeded and quartered
2 ounces white wine
6 ounces chicken stock
2 ounces asparagus, 1 inch pieces, blanched
2 ounces herbs, fresh (basil, parsley, chive)
¼ ounces white pepper
¼ ounces table salt

Heat sauté pan to high heat. Place oil in pan and sauté garlic until brown. Add shrimp and tomatoes immediately. Add white wine.

Reduce white wine and add stock. Remove from heat momentarily.

Cook linguini in boiling salted water until al dente. Just before linguini is finished, add asparagus to water to heat up. Strain pasta and asparagus, do not rinse.

Add pasta to the sauté pan with shrimp, etc. Toss with herbs, salt and pepper, and more olive oil. Serve and enjoy.

Photo courtesy of Miramar Bistro

sweets, treats & other eats

maple sugar candies

Bill McKibben, author, educator, founder of 350.org
Ripton, VT

2 cups fancy or light amber syrup
1 tablespoon butter

Equipment Needed:
Medium pot
Spoon
Candy thermometer
Flexible rubber molds

Start with about 2 cups of "fancy" or "light amber" syrup. The darker "Grade B" syrup, while better on pancakes, doesn't work as well for candy.

Put the candy thermometer on the edge of the pot. Add butter to the syrup and cook over medium heat.

Watch the candy thermometer closely. When the syrup reaches 240°F turn off the heat and let it cool.

When it cools to 160°F (which takes a few minutes), take a large metal spoon and stir it fast, until (quite suddenly) the consistency and color change—it will get lighter and thicker, with an almost plastic quality. Now you need to pour it quickly into the rubber molds.

It won't take long to cool, and when they do you just pop them out and eat them. Or, as we do, send them to your friends with a note saying you're thinking of them at the holidays, and that you've made a donation in their name to some group that's fighting climate change.

"Maple syrup is such a good food for thinking about global warming because its production is entirely dependent on weather. Maple trees only give their sap on those spring days when the nighttime temperature has been below 32°F but the day is above freezing. In recent years the season has shifted much earlier in the year; it used to be late March, but some sugar makers have harvested as early as January. Unless we get global warming under control, maple syrup will be a thing of the past in climates like ours. This would be a great sadness because it tastes delicious—and because it's great fun to wander the woods collecting the buckets of sap from the trees."

—Bill McKibben

Each December, my wife (the writer Sue Halpern), our daughter Sophie, and I make a batch of holiday presents for friends all around the country. We want to share some of the sense of our homeplace in the mountains above Lake Champlain, so we use the maple syrup we worked with our neighbors to make in the spring. The ingredient list is very short, but it is a bit of a chemistry project—it will take you a few batches to get it just right, but your mistakes will be quite delicious!

–Bill McKibben

Todd Stern's pancakes

Todd Stern, U.S. State Department Special Envoy for
Climate Change
Washington, D.C.

1½ cups flour
 1 teaspoon salt
 1 teaspoon sugar
1¾ teaspoons double-acting baking
     powder
 3 egg whites, lightly beaten
2½ tablespoons margarine or butter,
     melted
1¼ cups milk (lowfat or soy work well)

Mix flour, salt, sugar, and baking powder. Add egg whites, margarine, and milk. The more milk you use, the thinner the pancakes. Drop onto a hot griddle, lightly greased or non-stick. Feel free to add blueberries, bananas, or chocolate chips. When bubbles begin to form on top, flip and continue cooking until lightly browned.

Whistle Creek chokecherry syrup

Geoff Walton, organic farmer and rancher
Big Timber, MT

 3 cups chokecherry juice
6½ cups sugar
 ¼ teaspoon almond extract

Pour juice into kettle. Add sugar. Stir to mix. Place over high heat. Bring to boil and stir constantly. Boil hard for one minute. Remove from heat, skim off top coating. Add extract.
Pour into sterilized hot jars . Fill to 1/8" from top. Place lids. Process in water bath for 5 minutes.
Remove from water and let the jars seal.

porridge a la Baffin Island

Jeff Goodell, contributing editor at *Rolling Stone* and author of *How to Cool the Planet*

2 cups of rolled oats
1 large chunk of arctic ice
1 handful of dried cranberries
1 handful of M & Ms (or other fine chocolate)
½ cup olive oil

Rapidly melt arctic ice in pan over ultralight backpacking stove (be careful not to let stove tip over and burn down tent).

Mix in rolled oats, cook for three minutes, stirring occasionally.
Add cranberries, M & Ms, and olive oil (for additional calories necessary to keep warm in sub-zero temperatures).

Cover and let stand for five minutes while rolling up sleeping bag, packing tent, etc.

lavender butter cookies

Jill Silverman Hough, author of *100 Perfect Pairings Cookbook* series & co-author of *The Clean Plates Cookbook*
Napa, CA

Cookies

- 3 cups all-purpose flour
- 1 tablespoon dried lavender flowers*
- ½ teaspoon baking powder
- ½ teaspoon salt
- 1 cup (2 sticks) unsalted butter, softened
- 1 cup sugar
- 1 large egg
- 1½ teaspoons pure vanilla extract

Icing

- 1 cup confectioner's sugar (or more)
- 1 large egg white**
- ¼ teaspoon lemon juice
  Food coloring (optional)

These easy-to-make, easy-to-love cookies were inspired by a day of wine tasting, including the lavender-licious Matanzas Creek Winery. After I shape the dough into two logs, I usually freeze one of them. That way, a second batch is even easier to make—just thaw, cut, and bake.

In a medium bowl, combine the flour, lavender, baking powder, and salt. Set aside.

In the bowl of an electric mixer, cream together the butter and sugar. Add the egg and vanilla, beating until smooth. With the mixer on low speed, add the flour mixture, stirring until just combined.

Turn the dough out onto a lightly floured surface and divide it in half. Shape each half into a log, about 1¾ inches in diameter and 8 inches long. Wrap the logs in plastic and refrigerate for at least 1 hour. (You can refrigerate the logs as long as overnight, or freeze them for up to several months. Thaw, if necessary, before proceeding.) Preheat the oven to 375°F. Line baking sheets with parchment paper.

Remove plastic and cut the logs into ⅜-inch slices. Arrange the slices on the prepared baking sheets, about ½ inch apart. Bake until just beginning to turn golden brown at the edges, 11 to 13 minutes. Place the baking sheets on a cooling rack and cool thoroughly before decorating with Icing (see recipe), if desired. Makes about 4 dozen cookies.

Icing

This icing is purposefully thin enough to drizzle. If you want a stiffer icing, use 1½ to 2 cups of confectioner's sugar.

In the bowl of an electric mixer, combine the sugar, egg white, and lemon juice on slow speed, mixing until thick and smooth. (You can also use a medium mixing bowl and a whisk.)

Color icing as desired. Use a pastry bag or a resealable bag with a corner snipped off to drizzle icing over cookies.

*Note: Dried lavender flowers are available at specialty food stores and in the bulk dried herbs and flowers section at many natural food stores. Besides using them in this recipe, you can sprinkle them into other baked goods and over roasting poultry. You can also mix them into a dried herb blend called *Herbes de Provence*.

**Note: If you're concerned about using raw egg whites, substitute with the equivalent amount of dried egg whites and water.

apple pandowdy

**Meredith Brokaw, author of *Big Sky Cooking*
New York City, NY/West Boulder Valley, MT**

Crust
- 1 cup all-purpose flour
- 10 tablespoons (1¼ sticks) unsalted butter
- 3 tablespoons ice water

Filling
- ¾ cup firmly packed brown sugar
- ½ cup apple juice
- 2 tablespoons freshly squeezed lemon juice
- 1 teaspoon ground cinnamon
- ½ teaspoon ground ginger
- ½ teaspoon ground nutmeg
- ⅛ teaspoon ground cloves
- 8 large Granny Smith apples (about 4 pounds), peeled, cored, and sliced ½ inch thick
- 2 tablespoons unsalted butter
  Cold water, for brushing
- 1½ tablespoons granulated sugar
  Whipped cream or vanilla ice cream for serving

This dessert is made in a pie plate and topped with a nonfancy crust—some might even say that it lacks style. The topping looks like a primitive quilt made up of casually placed squares. An informal pie like this can be a hit even with fashionable eaters. The spices in the juice that the apples steep in also bathe the crust.

For the crust:
Place the flour and butter in the bowl of a food processor. Pulse on and off until the dough resembles coarse meal, 5 to 6 times. Add the ice water and pulse briefly until the dough forms a ball. On a lightly floured surface, roll the dough to a ¼-inch-thick rectangle, about 9 to 12 inches. Cut into twelve 3-inch squares and transfer to a cookie sheet; cover lightly with plastic wrap or a thin clean towel. Refrigerate for at least 30 minutes or overnight.

Preheat the oven to 425° F. Butter a deep 12 × 10-inch baking dish (or similar size).

For the filling:
In a medium bowl, combine the brown sugar, apple juice, lemon juice, cinnamon, ginger, nutmeg, and cloves. Add the apples and toss to combine. Spoon the mixture into the baking dish and dot with butter.

Arrange the chilled dough squares on top of the apples, overlapping them in a casual way. Brush the squares with cold water and sprinkle with the granulated sugar. Bake until the pandowdy starts to bubble and the crust is lightly browned, about 30 minutes. With a bulb baster, baste the crust with the juices from the bottom of the baking dish. Return the pandowdy to the oven and bake until the top is quite golden, about 30 minutes longer. Remove and let cool before serving with whipped cream or ice cream.

Photo by Emily Abrams

Relax. To be kind to the earth, you don't need to become a card-carrying member of PETA, an ice cream-shunning vegan, or even a no-meat-never-ever believer. Instead, you can be a "flexitarian"—in other words, an "almost" or "part-time" vegetarian. Big-name advocates of the trend include green foodies like Mark Bittman (*How to Cook Everything Vegetarian*), Deborah Madison (*Vegetarian Cooking for Everyone*), and Mollie Katzen (*Moosewood Cookbook*). Sure, they still cheerlead for diets rich in fruit, veggies, and nuts—but they say just cutting back on meat is good for your health and good for the planet.

It's easy to do, too. Mainstream grocery stores now carry soy milk, veggie burgers, and tofu—because their customers want alternatives to eating dairy and ground beef 24/7. In fact, 4 percent of Americans never consume meat, fish, or poultry (that is, anything with a face), and 47 percent eat at least one vegetarian meal a week, according to a 2012 national poll by Harris and the Vegetarian Resource Group. Purists may grumble. But the truth is, the new flexitarians are taking one giant green step for mankind.

—Karen Springen

flexitarian pecan pie

Karen Springen, journalist
Highland Park, IL

Pie Crust
1 ⅓ cups flour
1 teaspoon salt
⅓ cup vegetable oil
2 tablespoons cold water

Filling
3 eggs
2 teaspoons vanilla extract
2 teaspoons maple extract
¾ cup granulated sugar
¼ cup light brown sugar
3 cups pecans

A reason to smile: dessert is vegetarian! And pecans are full of protein. Typically pecan pie recipes call for loads of butter. This one doesn't ask for any. After all, the pecans themselves contain fat (the healthy kind). You won't notice the difference. Trust me.

Prepare a 9-inch pie crust of your choice. The easiest recipe, adapted from Betty Crocker, doesn't even require rolling or butter! Mix flour, salt, vegetable oil (such as canola), and cold water—in that order—and pat it into your pie pan.

Preheat oven to 375°F.

For the filling, mix eggs with 2 teaspoons vanilla and maple extract, ¾ cup granulated sugar, ¼ cup light brown sugar, and 3 cups of pecans. (Pecan lovers, go for 4 cups!)

Bake for about 45 minutes. Cool on a cooling rack.

summer berry torte

**James A. Lovell, Jr., astronaut, & James A. Lovell, III,
chef de cuisine, Lovell's Restaurant
Lake Forest, IL**

9 ounces sugar
9 ounces butter, cut into cubes, keep cool
9 ounces sliced almonds, toasted
3 ounces all-purpose flour
6 whole large eggs
2 pints blueberries
3 ounces apricot jam
1 pint blackberries
1 pint raspberries
1 pint strawberries
  Powdered sugar

Butter one 10-inch heavy-duty cake pan and line with parchment paper; dust with 1 teaspoon sugar.

Combine sugar, butter, almonds, and flour in a food processor. Process until a coarse meal forms.

Add eggs slowly, one at a time, processing until smooth.

Pour half of the batter into the prepared cake pan. Sprinkle the blueberries evenly over the batter and then pour in the rest of the batter.

Place in 350°F oven until toothpick comes out of the center clean.

Flip torte out of pan onto a wire rack; let cool to room temperature.

Spread the apricot jam over the top of the torte. Start with the blackberries and line the outside edge of the torte all around. Next use the raspberries and go around the inside of the blackberries. Slice the strawberries and overlap them to form a flower at the center of the torte.

Dust with a little sugar, and then with a lot of powdered sugar just before serving.

On Christmas Eve, 1968, the astronauts of Apollo 8 did a live broadcast from lunar orbit. So **Frank Borman, Jim Lovell, William Anders—the first humans to orbit the moon—**described what they saw, and they read Scripture from the Book of Genesis to the rest of us back here. And later that night, they took a photo that would change the way we see and think about our world. It was an image of Earth—beautiful; breathtaking; a glowing marble of blue oceans, and green forests, and brown mountains brushed with white clouds, rising over the surface of the moon.

And while the sight of our planet from space might seem routine today, imagine what it looked like to those of us seeing our home, our planet, for the first time. Imagine what it looked like to children like me. Even the astronauts were amazed. **"It makes you realize," Lovell would say, "just what you have back there on Earth."**

And around the same time we began exploring space, scientists were studying changes taking place in the Earth's atmosphere. Now, scientists had known since the 1800s that greenhouse gases like carbon dioxide trap heat, and that burning fossil fuels release those gases into the air. That wasn't news. But in the late 1950s, the National Weather Service began measuring the levels of carbon dioxide in our atmosphere, with the worry that rising levels might someday disrupt the fragile balance that makes our planet so hospitable. And what they've found, year after year, is that the levels of carbon pollution in our atmosphere have increased dramatically.

That science, accumulated and reviewed over decades, tells us that our planet is changing in ways that will have profound impacts on all of humankind.

—Excerpt from President Obama's speech at Georgetown University, June 25, 2013

the greener the better!

—The Daily Sip Bottlenotes

Everyone from winemakers to the sales clerks at Whole Foods is talking about "green" wine and it can get confusing. So we're here to break it down for you. Any wine made in an environmentally responsible manner can be called "green," but there are a few actual certifications that can make that term more meaningful.

Organic: This term can apply to the grape-growing process (no chemical fertilizers, pesticides, or herbicides or genetic engineering are used) or the winemaking process (no preservatives are used, such as sulfur dioxide). There are several organic certification programs in the U.S. and each one has its own rules. The "Organic" seal from the USDA promises 95% organic ingredients, while the "100% Organic" seal from the USDA indicates 100% organic ingredients. Both allow only naturally occurring sulfites in small quantities. The label "Made with Organic Grapes," means the wine contains at least 70% organic ingredients, and may include artificial sulfites.

Biodynamic: These wines are organic by default because biodynamic wineries approach the vines, soil and critters that live in the vineyard as parts to a whole, and no chemicals are used. Some practices include burying a cow horn full of manure over the winter then digging it up in the spring and mixing the manure with water to spray over the vineyard, and timing activities in the vineyard to the cycles of the moon. The theory was put forth by Austrian philosopher Rudolf Steiner in the 1920s, and many top-tier wineries now swear by the practice.

Sustainable: A sustainable wine may or may not be organic. The word means that the wine is produced in a manner that allows for healthy future production of grapes and wine, which often involves preventing soil erosion, avoiding harsh chemicals and water pollution. There are sustainable wine certification programs in many states, so check online for each state's specific guidelines.

Fish Friendly: There are many organizations dedicated to preserving the health of local fish, such as California's Fish Friendly Farming Program, which protects steelhead trout and Coho salmon in Northern California, or Salmon-Safe in Oregon, Washington and California. One of these labels on a bottle means that the winery works to improve water quality and the wildlife habitat on its property.

carrot & spice cake

Trish Karter, co-founder of Dancing Deer Baking Company
Boston, MA

Dry Mix

1½ cups all-purpose flour
½ cup white whole wheat flour
2 teaspoons baking powder
1 teaspoon baking soda
1 teaspoon fine-grain sea salt (I use Himalayan ground very fine)
1½ teaspoons cinnamon
½ teaspoon ground clove
½ teaspoon nutmeg
¼ teaspoon mace
1 whole ground whole fresh nutmeg
1 teaspoon ground coriander

Wet Mix

1 tablespoon finely ground lemon or orange peel
1 square inch fresh ginger
1 whole very ripe banana
1½ cups safflower or canola oil
1 cup granulated sugar
½ cup lightly packed brown sugar
1 tablespoon vanilla
4 whole large eggs
4 cups fresh shredded carrots
½ cup pecans, ground roughly
½ cup walnuts, ground roughly

This cake is really yummy, moist, very forgiving, and pretty darn healthy with lots of nutrients and protein. I amped it up a bit relative to most carrot cake nutritionally at no cost to the culinary satisfaction. As noted below, you can add and subtract ingredients, or go a bit heavier and lighter according to your taste, and it's still likely to be wonderful. I use as many organic ingredients as I can find but it doesn't change the taste if you can't find them. Good fresh carrots make a difference. If you love a really strong spice cake you can double these spices and it still works. Instead of frosting I serve squares of it with the best Greek yogurt I can find (preferably the real strained stuff you can find in the authentic Greek markets). See other serving suggestions below.

Heat oven to 350°F. Grease 13 x 9-inch baking pan with butter
(I like the flavor it adds). Coat lightly with flour.

Whisk together flours, baking powder and soda, dry spices, and salt in large bowl; set aside.

In a food processor fitted with a large shredding disk, shred the carrots (you should have about 4 cups, not packed); transfer the carrots to a bowl and set aside.

Take out the shredding disk and replace with the metal blade. Lightly grind the nuts to a course grind (don't grind too fine or the nut flour will make the batter heavy—better to have suspended bits of nuts). Remove the nuts and place them with the carrots.

Now in the same bowl (no need to clean in between) blend the granulated and brown sugars, eggs, vanilla, orange zest, ginger, and ripe banana until frothy and thoroughly

combined, about 20 seconds. With the
machine running, add the oil through the
feed tube in a steady stream. Continue
blending until the mixture is light in
color and well emulsified, at least 20
seconds longer.

Scrape the egg and sugar mixture into
the flour bowl. Add the carrots and nuts
and stir ingredients until incorporated
and no streaks of flour remain.

Pour into the prepared pan and bake until
a toothpick or skewer inserted into the
center of the cake comes out clean, 35
to 40 minutes, rotating the pan halfway
through the baking time.

Cool the cake to room temperature in the
pan on a wire rack, about 2 hours.

chocolate beet cake with hard crack glaze

Mary and Brenda Maher of The Cakegirls

For the cake:
- ½ cup vegetable oil
- 1½ cups dark brown sugar
- 2 cups pureed red beets (from 4 to 5 beets)
- ½ cup bittersweet chocolate chips, melted
- 1 teaspoon vanilla
- 1 cup all purpose flour
- ⅔ cup whole wheat flour
- ⅓ cup dutch cocoa powder
- 2 teaspoons baking powder
- ½ teaspoon salt

For the glaze:
- ½ cup chocolate chips
- 2 teaspoons vegetable oil

Trim root and stem end off of each beet and wrap each tightly in foil. Place them on a foil-lined tray and roast in a 400°F oven until tender when squeezed, 60-90 minutes depending on size. Cool completely in the foil. Unwrap and run each beet under cool water to easily slip off the skin. Cut the beets in chunks and puree in a food processor.

Lower oven to 375°F and coat a 6 cup Bundt pan with baking spray.

In a mixing bowl, mix oil and brown sugar until well combined. Add beets, melted chocolate chips, and vanilla and mix well.

In a separate bowl, stir together the flours, cocoa powder, baking powder, baking soda, and salt. Add the dry ingredients to the wet and stir until combined. Pour into prepared pan and spread batter out evenly. Bake for 35-40 minutes until toothpick inserted near the center comes out clean. Cool for 10 minutes before removing from the pan. Cool completely on a wire rack before glazing.

Melt the chocolate chips in the microwave. Remove and stir in the oil until smooth. Pour over the top of the cake. Once the glaze cools it will become firm or you can place the cake in the fridge to speed up the cooling time.

orange-cicle ice cream

**Manda Aufochs Gillespie, author of *The Green Mama*
Vancouver, Canada**

1/3 cup raw honey
2 cups orange juice
1/4 teaspoon orange extract
1 teaspoon vanilla extract
2 cups organic raw cream or whole
  milk
2 cups whole milk yogurt

Mix honey and orange juice together over low heat until somewhat concentrated. Add the extracts.
Mix the cream or milk and yogurt. Then blend both combinations together. Pour into your ice-cream maker. This is a delicious, refreshing, and nostalgic treat for a summer day without any of the added synthetic food coloring, preservatives, or low-quality dairy typical of many ice creams.

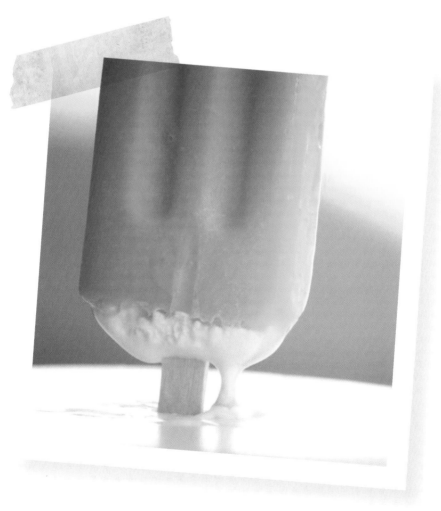

Moms today have more education than ever, but never has eating healthy seemed so complicated. Today, eating healthy takes time, money, and label-reading skills. Yet, you can forget all of this and just focus on one thing. **Eat real food.** That means food in its whole, unprocessed, and unpackaged state. Food that your grandma ate when she was little: eggs, butter, greens, beans, apples. Don't be tricked: your great grandma wasn't serving go-gurts, margarine, packaged breakfast cereal, goldfish crackers, rice crackers, 2% milk, soymilk, or margarine.

 Isn't it amazing when science recommends what your tongue always told you? The yummier stuff is actually better for you.

—Manda Aufochs Gillespie

my mom's chocolate chip cookies (my friends will do anything for these!)

Wendy Abrams, founder of Cool Globes (a.k.a. my mom)
Highland Park, IL

2 sticks butter
¾ cup brown sugar
⅔ cup white sugar
2 eggs
1 teaspoon vanilla
1 teaspoon baking soda
1 teaspoon salt
2⅔ cups flour
2 cups chocolate chips

Soften butter in microwave to the point where it is easy to blend without lumps, but not liquid; set aside.

Put brown sugar and white sugar into a mixing bowl. Stir in the butter and mix well with a wooden spoon. (If you use a hand mixer the batter and the cookies will be thinner.) Add in eggs; stir. Add in vanilla, baking soda, and salt; stir. Mix in 1 cup of the flour; stir. Add in the rest of the flour, and stir. Pour in chips, stir.

Bake at 325°F. The key to baking the best cookies is taking them out of the oven at precisely the right time (and this will vary from oven to oven). Take them out as soon as they no longer look "wet" but before they are brown. They will look undercooked, but they will continue to bake for a few minutes on the hot cookie sheet when you take them out of the oven.

homemade challah

Mayor Rahm Emanuel
Chicago, IL

1 package rapid rise yeast
2 teaspoons sugar
4½ cups bread flour
2 large eggs
⅓ cup sugar
⅓ cup canola oil
1½ teaspoons salt
¾ cup warm water
1 egg for egg wash prior to baking

Dissolve rapid rise yeast with ⅔ cup warm water. Let sit for about 5 minutes.

Put flour in mixer, make a well, and add eggs, sugar, oil, salt, water, and yeast mixture. Mix on low just until ingredients are incorporated (about 30 seconds).

Change mixer to the dough hook and knead for about 5 minutes. Add more flour if needed.

Place dough in an oiled bowl and cover with a towel. Let dough rise for 1½ - 2 hours.

Punch the dough down. Braid the dough into 1 big or 2 small loaves. Place braids on greased (or sil-pat) baking sheet and cover and let rise for 30–60 minutes.

Brush tops of loaves with egg wash (1 egg + 1 tablespoon water). Sprinkle with poppy or sesame seeds, if desired. Bake at 350°F for 30-40 minutes.

"Chicago is healthier and more economically vibrant as we work to reduce our emissions. There are tremendous benefits in increasing energy efficiency in buildings—saving dollars, creating jobs, making buildings more comfortable, and reducing our emissions."

— Mayor Rahm Emanuel, Chicago, IL

chocolate raspberry swirl cheesecake

Cassie Pierson, pastry chef
Highland Park, IL

Crust
- 1 cup walnuts, ground to a fine powder
- 3 tablespoons coconut sugar
- 2 tablespoons cacao powder
- 2 tablespoons coconut oil

Filling
- 1½ cups cashews
- ¾ cup almond milk
- 1½ cups raspberries
- ¼ cup coconut nectar (or other liquid sweetener)
- 2 tablespoons lemon juice
- 2 tablespoons beet juice (optional, for color)
- ⅓ cup coconut oil, melted

Topping
- ¾ cup cacao powder
- 2 tablespoons coconut oil
- 2 tablespoons coconut nectar (or other liquid sweetener)
- 3 tablespoons almond milk

Mix the walnuts, coconut sugar, cacao powder, and coconut oil by hand. In a lined spring-form cheesecake pan press the dough into a "shortbread" crust.

To make the cheesecake filling, blend the cashews, almond milk, raspberries, coconut nectar, lemon juice, beet juice, and the coconut oil in a high speed blender (such as a Vitamix) until smooth. Be sure to add the oil last.

Remove and reserve one cup to the side before adding the cacao powder, coconut oil, coconut nectar, and almond milk and blending again.

Pour the chocolate layer over the crust and spread evenly. Pouring in a circular motion, add the remaining cup of blended raspberry filling on top. Use a toothpick to delicately swirl the raspberry and chocolate layers together. Put the cheesecake in the freezer and allow it to set overnight. Thaw before serving.

Take a dash of hope,
a small pinch of pride
in your country . . .
mix with the yearning
for a better world for
your children, add a
little love and peace...
stir and voila...soul
food.

—Graham Nash

Index